THE
NEW AGE
PRIMER

Spiritual Tools For Awakening

The
New Age
Primer

The
New Age
Primer

Published by
Light Technology Publishing
P.O. Box 1526
Sedona, AZ 86339

ISBN 0-929385-48-9

Book Concept by Glen Phillips
Cover Art by Delmary
Cover Design by Fay Richards

Printed in the United States of America
Mission Possible Commercial Printing
P.O. Box 1495
Sedona, AZ 86339
                              10 9 8 7 6 5 4 3 2 1

We gratefully acknowledge Glen Phillips'
conceptual and financial contributions
to the New Age Primer

This book is dedicated
to Glen's late wife

Helen Joan Phillips

Table of Contents

Introduction, *Glenn Phillips*

1. Your Birthright is to Be a Free Soul, *Pete Sanders Jr.* 1

2. Reincarnation: Fact or Fantasy? *Patricia-Rocelle Diegel* 27

3. The Chakras, *Hallie Deering* 37

4. What is Channeling? *Vywamus/Barbara Burns* 43

5. Meditation for Everyone, *The Beings of Light/Ruth Ryden* 61

6. Spirit Guides, *Ai Gvhdi Waya* 71

7. Walk with the Angels: Aliens and ETs, *Rev. Helga Morrow* 85

8. UFOs: A Case in Point, *Virgil Armstrong* 89

9. Astrology, *Marilyn Warram* 95

10. Numerology, *Lynn Buess* 105

11. The Tarot, *Marlene Ayers-Johnston* 119

12. Palmistry, *Marlene Ayers-Johnston* 125

13. Earth Changes Create Body Changes
    Speaks of Many Truths/Robert Shapiro 133

14. Crystals, *Dorothy Roeder* 155

15. Life Behind Sleep, *Marlene Myhre* 171

16. Rebirthing, *Alice Tickner* 179

17. Creative Visualization, *Glenn Phillips* 187

18. Beliefs Can Heal Your Life, *Louise Hay* 195

Introduction

Welcome to the New Age. This book is directed primarily toward the newcomer to the thinking of this era which is changing the way we view our new realities. Although the book was conceived and written with the novice in mind, there is something in it for all of us, as we are all on the road to discovery and self-awareness together.

The idea for this book came to me while I was browsing through a bookstore in Sedona, Arizona. It was my third or fourth New Age bookstore in as many days, and my mind was starting to go into overload at the many subjects and authors available. I was baffled by the task of trying to keep my selections down to what I could afford, to say nothing of what I had room to carry home. I have been on this road to self-awareness for a number of years, but I began to wonder how anyone just starting to take that first tentative step toward enlightenment and the New Age could ever possibly make a selection from among this smorgasbord of delicacies laid out before me.

I remembered back to when I had taken that first tentative step myself. I was desperate to read anything and everything I could get my hands on that had anything remotely to do with what I thought I was striving toward.

All too often I found myself plodding through two or three hundred pages of a book that I was not ready for. I found myself reading about past-life regressions when what I really was "into" at that time was channeling or meditating. I have never read a self-awareness book that I didn't get something out of but quite often I have found myself wading into a book and then having to put it aside until later when I was ready for it.

I hope that this book will help. It is what the title suggests — an introduction to what is out there for the interested reader. Some of the authors you are about to read are professional writers, while others are being published for the first time, but one thing is common to all of them: they are all knowledgeable in their own fields. We have deliberately kept the list of topics relatively short to allow the writers enough space to explain their subjects clearly and, I hope, to pique your interest. For those interested in continuing with any given subject, a list of recommended titles is offered at the end of most chapters.

I ask only that you read this book with an open mind and a positive heart. Remember always that there is no single truth. There are many truths and many paths, and I hope that within the pages of this book you find the truths and the paths that "feel right" for you. Enjoy.

Glenn Phillips
April 1993

1

Your Birthright Is to Be a Free Soul

Pete A. Sanders Jr.

Of all the important and valuable things in life, nothing is more precious than happiness. Happiness is the elusive butterfly that people around the world pursue through their lifetimes. Some try to find it in material wealth or possessions. Others try to find it in success or achievement. Still others try to find it in family, friends and the other people around them.

Sooner or later a person comes to realize that happiness comes from within, from the feelings of fulfillment gained by understanding oneself and the process of life. Many people achieve small glimpses of this fulfillment by mastering parts of the world around them, either in their homes, in school or in business. That fulfillment, and consequently its related happiness, soon fade, however, when people are removed from their area of mastery or understanding. Further, many successful people finally realize that even total mastery of their area of endeavor or specialty still leaves them unsatisfied and unhappy. Seeking happiness from things outside the self ultimately doesn't work.

Demonstrate this to yourself physically with this symbolic analogy. Hold up your right hand and try to touch your right arm with that hand. Really give it a try. Pretend that if you can do it you will have achieved happiness. It is hard work, isn't it, and your results are usually less than totally successful. Feel the tension, stress and unpleasant feelings that this effort generates. This is what it is like when you strive to find happiness outside of yourself.

The solution lies in becoming a master of yourself and finding

Figure 1

happiness in realizing that your hand is always touching your arm at the wrist. Hold your hand up again and feel where it naturally joins your arm. Feel how much easier it is to be at peace with the connection and contact you already have. This is what it is like when you let your happiness flow from within.

You are the one common element in every phase of your life and living experience. You are a major factor in every moment of your day. Once you learn to master yourself, you carry that complete inner security and joy of living into everything you do.

This is not a new concept. "Know thyself" has been a watchword often repeated through the ages. For all its repetition, however, its potential remains one of the least explored fields in society today. Mastery of self means understanding and realizing your complete potential and capabilities, knowing the unlimitedness that you can be. The short verse associated with Figure 1 symbolizes the spirit of the freedom to control your own destiny that comes from fully understanding yourself and your true nature.

All of your life you have been taught to think of yourself as primarily a body or physical being. Schools and other institutions concentrate on teaching only physical or physically related skills: reading, speaking, athletics, business and so forth. The myriad forms of advertisements and commercials promote products that focus only on the physical, such as clothes, cosmetics, hair care and hygiene products. Those of you fortu-

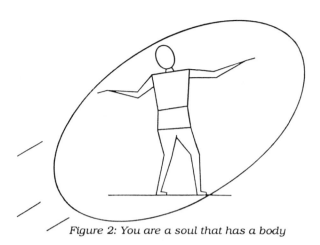

Figure 2: You are a soul that has a body

nate enough to have received some form of religious or spiritual training may at least have been taught that you have a soul that goes with the physical being you call your body. That instruction for many people is actually a further cause of limitations. You do not have a soul.

The reality is not that you are a body or that you have a soul. The truth is that you *are* a soul. You are a soul that has a body. The real you, your true self, is that soul nature. This article will help you to experience for yourself the unlimited potentials and freedom for growth that are your birthright as that Free Soul.

Figure 1 illustrates you, the full you (body and soul nature), in your journey through life and learning in our universe. The moving circle above the head of the figure standing for your body represents your soul nature, the real you, the "you soul" (as opposed to your soul: remember, you are a soul, you do not have a soul). This concept is sometimes better represented by Figure 2, where the symbol for the soul nature includes and encloses within it the symbol for your body. You are both the body and the soul, but the soul is by far the major and most important part of your being. Because it is pure energy, the soul is the part of you that is not only unlimited but is also everlasting.

I am sure that soul is a term most of you are comfortable with. All major religions include within their framework the concept of the soul. Whether it is called soul, spirit, atman or intelligent energy, the meaning is still the same. From a scientific point of view, you may think of the soul as being a unique energy pattern or field that lies beyond the transience of physical matter and outside the limited forms of currently measurable energy. In terms of the revolutionary Superstring Theory of physics, the soul could be those additional six dimensions science is now saying we all have.

The technique below represents a first step in exploring your soul nature for yourself. It is based on learning a pathway for shiftIng your focus back to the soul from your normally more body-oriented perspective.

If you had to designate a three-dimensional location for the energy that is the real you, the soul, it would be an area above and slightly behind the head. This is why paintings of saints and religious figures locate a halo there. It is also the reason why most people first see the aura around the head area. (It is not actually the body's energy field, but the soul's energy field they are seeing.)

An approximate visual analogy for the relationship of the soul energy to the body would be to think of an upside-down iceberg. Most people are aware of how the most massive part of an iceberg lies below the water and only a small portion of it extends above the water. If you turned that picture upside down, you would have a good analogy for the relationship of the soul energy to the body. Most of the energy that you are as a soul actually exists outside of the body (in that area above and slightly behind the head), like that massive underwater portion of the iceberg. The small portion of the iceberg above the water is similar to an extension of the soul that comes down into the body, hooks up with the brain and the central nervous system, and runs the physical machinery.

Most of your life you have been trained to focus your awareness down through that energy connection and out through the physical senses. In the technique described below you turn that focus back inward (becoming more aware of your body than your environment), shift your focus up through your body to the head area, and make a final focus shift up and out into that soul energy.

Most people experience this final focus shift as the boundaries disappearing or as stepping into a bigger room. Experience this soul-shift for yourself. Remember to guide your focus gently rather than forcing or overconcentrating.

Making the Soul-Shift

Procedure:

1. Relax, sit comfortably and close your eyes. Initially do not try to be aware of anything specific. Go ahead and note what you are feeling, sensing and experiencing from yourself and your environment.

2. Gradually increase your awareness of yourself rather than of your environment. Do not try to concentrate, but instead gently focus your awareness on what you are feeling from and within yourself.

3. When you have attained and are maintaining a higher level of awareness of yourself than of your surroundings, begin to become more aware of your lower legs. Feel your feet, your ankles, your calves, and begin to shift your focus up through each part of your body. As you sense each body area in turn and are moving upward, gradually leave behind the parts you have already sensed and slowly tune them out, letting your awareness of them blend into your awareness of yourself as a whole. Continue this process until you reach the head area.

4. As you focus more specifically on the head area, take the time to feel all the thoughts and memories that are you. Briefly, just let yourself go and see what comes to mind when you focus on yourself as a person.

5. Holding these same thoughts and feelings of yourself as a person, shift your focus one more level upward to that soul area. (Many people experience this final focus shift as a feeling of stepping back and out of the top of their heads.) Feel that same awareness you had of you as a person (when you were focusing on the head area) grow deeper, as if you had stumbled onto a richer part of yourself that you have seldom explored. Feel how the boundaries fall away and your being becomes more unlimited. It may even feel as though you have slipped between the cracks into a deeper, more expansive dimension. This is the real you. You have become aware of your soul nature.

Note:

If you feel any pressure in your forehead or eye area as you make that final focus shift, you are probably trying to turn your eyes backward and force them to look out of the back of your head. They

will not go there. Leave them where they belong. Make that final
focus shift more as a feeling of letting your mind float or as a
heightened awareness of the space above you.

6. Now take the time to experience the feeling and beingness that
are this full you, your soul nature. Note how different it feels (deeper,
more aware, stronger than your normal awareness during daily life).
Explore the greater expansiveness and wider boundaries of this more
extensive you.

7. One last time, capture in your mind the full feeling of your soul
nature; then gently shift your focus back down to the head area and
note some specific part of your body (nose, mouth, hands). Slowly
move a finger or foot, and when you feel ready, open your eyes.
Gently move your body to restore your normal physical orientation.

Summary:

With this technique you have taken the first step on a long and
fascinating journey into the expanded dimensions of soul consciousness. The more you meditate and practice soul awareness, the easier
it will become for you to tune out your environment and the distrac-
tions of the body. Also, the more you experience and learn to identify
your soul nature, the easier it will become to make that final, up-and-
out focus shift. The technique can also be used at any time as a
relaxer. When you are tense and under stress from the events of the
day, you can soul-shift and quickly unwind. After you have learned
greater control, soul-shifting can also serve as a meditation for greater
self-understanding and exploration.

As a side note, when you make that final focus shift, your level of
alpha brain-wave activity increases markedly. Many people think that
an increased alpha brain pattern is the cause of paranormal abilities,
when actually it is only the result of tapping (consciously or uncon-
sciously) the soul.

Why is the concept that you are a soul so important? Because if
you are a soul, then you are all the unlimited potentials that are that
soul nature. As illustrated in Figure 3, the soul has the ability to tap
unlimited beingness to expand, blend and become one with every
aspect of the universe. Further, the soul is also unlimited in its ability
to travel to, explore in and learn from every part of the cosmos.

The body by comparison is extremely limited by its physical nature
alone. What a tragedy it would be to take on the physical limitations

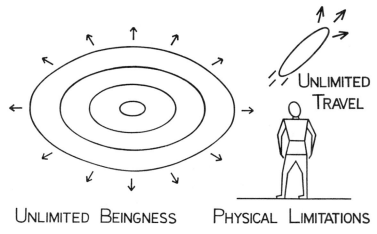

UNLIMITED BEINGNESS   PHYSICAL LIMITATIONS

*Figure 3: The unlimited potentials of the soul
contrasted with the limitations of the body*

of your body and apply them to your total being and spirit. Your birthright is to experience not only the joy and freedom that come from knowing you are a soul, but also to explore and develop your unlimited potentials in all phases of your life.

Let's experience a beginning form of tapping the soul's unlimited potentials. The technique described below introduces you to the soul's ability to blend and be one with all things. We call this "soul-blending." See for yourself how easy it is, once you know how.

Soul-Blending

Procedure:

1. Sit comfortably and close your eyes. Breathe calmly and then shift your focus up to your soul energy.

2. Gently relax and enjoy the feeling of you, your soul nature. After a short while, allow that awareness to expand so that it gradually includes your whole body as well. Feel the real you becoming one with your physical body. Feel your body melt and blend into your awareness of yourself. At this point you may be experiencing for the first time the complete fullness of your total being (body, mind and soul). You should feel like one big ball of awareness, extending beyond the limits of your body but also penetrating deeper into the fabric of your physical self than you normally experience.

3. Next, allow your awareness, your being, to expand again so that

it gradually includes all of the chair you are sitting in. Feel your arms melting into the arms of the chair; feel your back gently sinking into the energy of the chair. Feel yourself and the chair becoming one, so that your awareness now includes yourself, your physical being and the chair.

4.   Once you feel at one with the chair, explore it. What does it feel like inside? Can you feel all its parts: legs, back, under the seat? Can you feel where the chair touches the floor or the carpet?

5.   Allow your awareness to expand again and blend along the carpet or the floor to all corners of the room. Sense the other objects that come in contact with the floor and blend with them. Explore.

6.   When you have finished exploring, gradually return your awareness to your physical body, open your eyes and gently move to restore your normal physical orientation.

Summary:

As with the soul-shift, a key emphasis in this technique is not to try or to force concentration, but rather to relax and flow. Gently guide yourself to where you want to go. Soul-blending with your body is an excellent physical relaxer. The process itself is also an automatic mental and spiritual relaxer, as it expands the usually tighter focus of your soul energy. You can soul-blend with any item that you can hold or make contact with. You can sense into it to check for damage and safety or merely to explore it from within. On your own you can extend into the energy of the entire world around you.

Another of the soul's unlimited potentials is the ability to tap into extrasensory perception. The psychic senses are the senses of the soul. They are the natural way that you as a soul perceive the world around you. Just as your body uses the physical senses to discern the physical aspects of your environment, the soul can perceive the nonphysical vibrations and communications that surround you. All that is required is knowledge of how these psychic/soul senses function and training in how to use them.

For too long you have been trained to use and trust only your physical senses. Some of you may even have been trained out of your psychic senses and told to ignore your feelings, hunches and impressions. All you need to reawaken your atrophied psychic senses is training. You too can become a pioneer on the frontier of the human psychic potential.

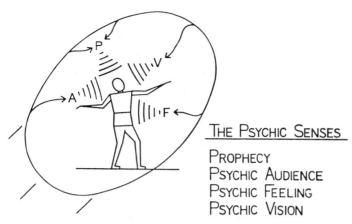

Figure 4: *The pyschic senses are the senses of the soul*

The soul has four main extrasensory channels for discerning the world around it. These comprise the four primary psychic senses: prophecy (or psychic intuition), psychic audience (hearing), psychic feeling, and psychic vision (Figure 4).

Psychic intuition, often called prophecy, is the psychic sense that the majority of people find the most phenomenal. It is usually thought of as knowing the future or being able to predict events. This is only one aspect of prophecy, however. This soul-sensing channel receives information as an inner knowing. It is the sense of just intuitively knowing without understanding how or why you know. These psychic intuition impressions can be about the past, the present or the future. What distinguishes perceptions received through prophecy from all others is the way they frequently come out of the blue. You just know, often with little supporting evidence to confirm the belief that the knowing is correct. Prophecy is also the psychic sense most closely associated with full trance.

Everyone has experienced at least minor examples of this form of ESP — knowing that someone would call or having a hunch or intuition about something. Married couples frequently know what their partner is thinking or may start to broach the same thought at the same time. Many people also receive small future insights and premonitions in their dreams. All these are small examples of psychic intuition and prophecy.

Psychic audience is the soul's sense of hearing, often called clair-audience (clear hearing). Through it impressions are received either as psychic hearing or in words. Clairaudient impressions can range from a strong, clear hearing, like a voice sounding inside your head, to its gentler forms which can be as subtle as a mental understanding that comes in language form. If you have ever been somewhere and thought you heard your name called but no one was there, or if at times ideas come to you as words, phrases or concepts that you understand or hear, you have experienced aspects of psychic audience.

Psychic hearing is frequently mistaken for talking to yourself because both use the same internal circuitry of the brain's temporal lobes. To tell the difference, notice your perception of where the sound originates. When you talk to yourself, your perception of the answering voice will usually tend to be on your left side, in the left-brain area, because this is the part of the brain that deals with language and language formation. Some people, particularly left-handers, notice the impression more on the right side. The side really doesn't matter, however. The main difference between talking to yourself and psychic hearing is that the latter seems to occur more in the center of your head. Also, the clairaudient impression will not necessarily be heard in your own voice. It will be a word, a phrase or language that's understood in a generic voice. When you talk to yourself, your answers are likely to be more in your own tone of voice and your personal speaking style.

Psychic feeling can be the most useful of the soul senses in daily life. It is easily the simplest to master. The main obstacle to applying the psychic senses practically is not learning how to sense psychically, but rather learning to interpret accurately what you are receiving. Impressions received through psychic feeling come simply as feelings or sensations. Most people can, by and large, accurately interpret the meanings of the feelings they receive. Those they are not familiar with can quickly be learned. For this reason psychic feeling is frequently the easiest form of ESP for most people to develop.

More often than not the question is more one of learning to pay attention to your feelings (to become aware of them). Our society tends to train us to ignore our feelings and rely solely on thinking or logic to function effectively. Men and career-oriented women are particularly victimized by this training. They are taught to be unemotional and logical, to suppress their feeling sensitivity.

It should be realized that there is a distinct difference between emotions and psychic feeling. Emotions are intense inner reactions, usually generated by strong mental processes or associations. In their intensity they can burst to the surface and override or control your actions. Psychic feelings are simply the natural way the soul senses its own environment. Inner feelings reflect your state of mind or being, and outer feelings carry information concerning the vibration or energy patterns of the environment and those in it.

To control the emotions and limit the extremes to which their excesses can drive your actions is indeed a valuable skill. To completely ignore or eliminate all feelings, however, is an unwise overreaction. It strips away a primary sensing and information-gathering channel. What is needed is to understand and constructively apply the information received through feelings. By opening your sensitivity to receiving psychic feeling impressions and fully understanding the messages they carry, you can vastly increase your awareness of the world around you.

Anyone who has walked into a room where there has been a disagreement and felt the tension in the air has experienced psychic feeling. Impressions received through this channel can range in intensity from strong physical sensations or even pain to the subtler feelings of a mood or an atmosphere. The gift of psychometry (receiving impressions through touching objects) is also primarily a function of the use of psychic feeling.

The fourth and last of the psychic senses is psychic vision, also known as clairvoyance (clear seeing). This is the sense that deals with receiving information as pictures, images, symbols and visual impressions. Psychic vision is also the primary sense utilized in seeing the aura (the energy field around the body). It is additionally responsible for the images and pictures you see in dreams.

Although frequently one of the most impressive and fascinating of the psychic senses, psychic vision is also the most difficult to utilize practically. Because many clairvoyant impressions are symbols or symbolic images, their meaning is not always clear or obvious. For this reason you need to know not only how to unfold your psychic vision but also how to interpret the information you receive.

Figure 5: The vision psychic reception area

If you have dreams or see pictures or images as you daydream or if you have ever had a picture or scene suddenly come to mind, you have experienced a minor aspect of psychic vision. You can develop and control this inner vision. You can psychically see the aura, or energy field, around the body.

Psychic Reception Areas

Most of this initial information about the psychic senses has been widely known for years. Humanity has been experiencing psychic sensitivity and investigating it for centuries. The practical control of ESP, however, has been inconsistent or limited to the select few with strong natural abilities.

However, you can trigger your ESP at will. Now a path has been opened to the very core of these psychic channels, gateways that will make it possible for you to use ESP as a daily way of life. Those gateways are called the "psychic reception areas."

The history of paranormal experiences is sufficiently documented that from current literature you can easily learn the "what" to look for in psychic perception. Descriptions of psychic occurrences and their impressions are abundant enough to provide a relatively accurate picture or type of signal to be open to. Your own personal experience with extrasensory episodes can also provide that background. Missing, however, have been the "where and how" of receiving psychic perceptions and a method for controlling and accessing these higher senses on demand, as a practical skill. The psychic reception areas are the vacuum. They are the catalytic keys for crossing the threshold to full psychic mastery.

What are these catalysts and how can they dramatically change your life? The psychic reception areas are specific locations on and around the body that serve as focal points for the four primary psychic senses. Just as the physical senses have points (the hands, eyes, ears, nose and mouth) on which you can focus to intensify your physical perceptions, so too the psychic senses have focal points that can increase and amplify your extrasensory abilities. Knowing the location of the psychic reception areas and how to contact them equips you with the ability to psychically "sense on command." You will be able to trigger ESP when you want to rather than randomly or seemingly not at all. Having this ability brings the same convenient versatility with ESP that you enjoy with the physical senses. It gives you the potential of doubling your information by having nine sources of input instead of only five. It opens the gateway for evolving beyond using only the physical senses. No longer will you have to hope that you can tune in psychically. Never again will you have to wonder if an extrasensory perception is accurate or has been interpreted correctly. The days of psychic sensitivity's being out of your reach are over. You have the means to become fully psychic.

Let's begin your psychic education with how to see an aura. To explore the world of aura vision, the first step is to identify the location of the psychic reception area for psychic vision. The first technique below helps you to specifically locate your "third eye," as the vision psychic reception area is frequently called. The second technique gives you a procedure for practicing aura vision.

Vision Focus-Shift

Procedure:

1. Relax and sit comfortably. Before pinpointing your exact vision psychic reception area, it is important to understand the foci or center points of both the physical and psychic vision fields. An awareness of how that center point shifts when you switch from physical vision to psychic vision is crucial for understanding and effectively utilizing your vision psychic reception area.

2. Begin by finding the center point of your physical vision field. Relax and look straight ahead. While looking at the entire scene in front of you, feel where the center of your vision field is in relation to your face. That is, if a perfectly straight and level line were extended back toward you from the center of your field of vision, where would that line touch your face? Most people find that the center of their physical vision field lies between their eyes and about an inch down from their eyebrows, at about the bridge of the nose.

3. Experiment to get a clear feeling of where your physical vision's center point is. If you are having difficulty, extend your arm, point a finger at yourself and with your eyes open gradually bring your finger closer and closer to you (keeping it in the center of your field of vision) until it touches your face. Do not stare at your finger. Look straight ahead and keep your finger in the center of what you see until it touches your face. This point is the center of your physical vision field.

4. Now find the center of your psychic vision field. Before proceeding, however, take a minute to sense fully the center of your physical vision field. Feel how you can identify this area and be aware of its existence. Now close your eyes. See if you notice any shift in your vision field or its center. Most people feel a slight but distinct upward shift, for when you close your eyes you will in most cases automatically switch from physical vision to psychic vision. With your eyes open you have both vision capabilities, but you usually ignore or are unaware of your psychic vision in favor of the physical vision you have been trained to use.

5. Open and close your eyes. See if you can feel the shift. Now, with your eyes closed try to feel the center of whatever visual perception you have, even if all you see is blackness. Most people find the center to be higher than their physical vision center — generally in an area of the forehead half an inch to an inch above the eyebrows. If you have difficulty feeling that center point, keep your eyes closed and bring your finger toward yourself until you touch your face. Try to keep your finger in the center of whatever you are perceiving with your eyes closed. It does not matter what you see, even if it is total darkness; just stay in the center of it. Developing your awareness of this vision-field and center-point shift is the key to understanding and using the vision psychic reception area. By focusing your visual attention more in this area you will find it easier to receive psychic visual impressions.

6. With your eyes open, gently shift your focus of visual attention up to the psychic reception area. See if you feel a greater awareness from or in this area of your visual field. Note your impressions and feelings and compare them with your experience when you look only with physical vision.

Summary:

Everyone will feel a slightly different center point for their physical and psychic vision fields. The important issue is not the exact location of these center points but rather the shift that occurs when you change from one vision field to the other. This shift demonstrates that you do have more than one visual capability. Once you master the shift you will have on-command ability to experience both aura vision and clairvoyance.

Remember to use the vision psychic reception area, not just your eyes, for the next technique.

Aura Vision

Procedure:

1. Note: This technique requires the involvement of other people. If you are doing the techniques by yourself, you will need to go where you can observe people, preferably people who are sitting still in front of a light background, or ask a volunteer to assist you.

2. If you are in a group, pick a volunteer from the group to sit in an open area in front of a light background (or hang a sheet behind the person).

3. Face the subject from about ten to twenty feet away. Become aware of your vision psychic reception area. Without looking at the person, relax and focus your awareness in the third-eye region of your forehead. Leave your eyes open, but shift your attention upward to your psychic vision.

4. When you feel in tune with your vision psychic reception area, observe the person in front of you. Let your eyes rest on the subject while you focus on your vision psychic reception area. If you do this properly, you will feel as if you are looking more from the level of your forehead than from the level of your eyes. Do not look directly at the person, but rather beyond or just slightly over his or her head. This naturally shifts your awareness upward to the third-eye area.

5. You will begin to see a thin (one- to three-inch) band of Light or

glow around the outline of the body. The effect will be strongest in the head and shoulder areas. This is how most people begin to see the aura, as a Light halo around the other person. The more you relax and the more your subject relaxes, the wider and more distinct this halo will become. Eventually you will be able to see colors and colored areas within this field as well as above the head and in front of the body.

Note:

As your aura vision is just beginning, these colors will be transparent in nature, very evanescent and easy to see through. Do not expect to see vivid, solid colors that completely obscure your view of the individual. Look more for a subtle color impression. Also, remember not to try or force concentration but rather to just relax and see what impressions you receive.

6. Rotate participants so that everyone gets at least two or three opportunities to view the auras of different individuals. Notice how some people's auras are wider than others and how different color patterns appear around each individual. The width or intensity of the aura can give you a good idea of people's level of relaxation as well as the vitality of their energy. The various colors can serve as clues to their basic characteristics and personality traits.

Summary:

This technique is your introduction to the vast field of aura vision. It is designed to help you see that first halo or transparent energy field around a person, with the colors and deeper impressions coming to you as you relax and become comfortable with the process. Increasing your aura vision ability is entirely up to you. The more you practice, the better and easier it will get. There are many situations at home or at work that can be utilized to improve your aura vision. Any place you can observe relatively motionless people, you can practice viewing their auras. By paying attention to the size and intensity of the aura, you can gauge how nervous or fatigued the individuals are. Any colors you sense can give you additional insight. Even in your beginning stages you can use your aura vision to tell you about people you deal with if you have a chance to view them briefly before interacting with them. As a minimum, you can observe the different shapes and energy patterns that reflect each person's unique aura.

Everyone Is Psychic

Everyone has all four of the psychic senses. Much of society is still under the misconception that only some people are psychic. This is a totally incorrect. The psychic senses are as much a part of everyone as is their soul nature. While it is true that some people are more naturally open to ESP, the difference in psychic abilities is usually more a function of each individual's different psychic strengths.

At this point, you might be saying, "If all this is true, why don't I exhibit more psychic abilities?" The answer is that you have actually been trained out of them. All your life you have been trained to identify only with your physical body and the limited physical potentials it possesses. If you compare the years of emphasis you have had on the body and its physical senses (walking, talking, reading, writing) with the lack of training you have received in experiencing your soul nature and its senses, it is not surprising that your psychic and soul capabilities are underdeveloped.

Do not misunderstand. The training you have received in using the body and its physical senses is by no means harmful or undesirable. You need these skills to live, work and exist here on Planet Earth. It is time, however, to develop psychic abilities as well. Without them you are automatically limited to only five senses instead of nine.

Another main source of limitation is the controlling effects of outside conditioning and programming. From birth, all of us are subject to at least some forms of behavior modification. Conditioning refers to the process whereby we learn to associate specific behaviors with receiving a reward (or sometimes avoiding punishment). The types of reward received can vary from food or gifts to love, acceptance and approval. Programming refers to the manner in which a series of conditioned habit patterns can cause you to consistently react or respond subconsciously, rather than acting consciously as a result of your own initiative and decisions.

Figure 6 illustrates how these outside pressures and influences gradually control us, forming a network of conditioned habit patterns and programmed responses that we feel we must or should follow. Many times these habit patterns and responses are so subtly ingrained that we carry them out almost subconsciously, never questioning why

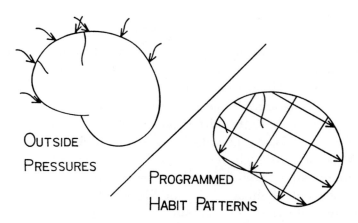

OUTSIDE
PRESSURES
                    PROGRAMMED
                    HABIT PATTERNS

Figure 6: Conditioning and programming habit-pattern formation

we are doing them but still frequently resenting their limiting influence and control. A typical example is the conditioning and programming of approval. One effect of this form of programming is the way people can feel compelled to gain the approval of someone who rejects them or acts hard to please.

This is just one of the many forms of conditioning and programming that shape, control and limit the action of the individual. These effects are felt in all areas of our lives. Advertising agencies play on these conditioned responses (the desire to be liked, to look attractive, to be admired) to induce people to purchase their products. Aspects of your personal or business life can also be markedly affected by your programming in the areas of appearance, approval, discipline and reaction to authority.

The final major source of our limitations is the general failure of society to recognize and understand the effects of environmental psychic pollution. Figure 7 illustrates some of these influences that can affect you daily.

The arrows represent the thoughts and feelings radiating from individuals around you that are directed at you from afar. Thoughts are things. They generate a vibration or energy pattern that can affect you. The negative effects do not come only from angry or hostile thoughts. Someone constantly thinking of, yearning for or worrying about you can also be highly disruptive. The vibration of

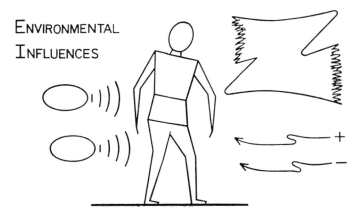

Figure 7: Disruptive psychic pollution — environmental influences

this constant thought energy is like being repeatedly interrupted. I'm sure you have experienced the feelings of tension, anxiety or disorganization that come when someone is worried about you or upset with you. It is also possible to pick up someone else's tension, depression or fatigue and take it on as your own. Those headaches that you can't shake or those "off" feelings that depress you may not even be yours.

A similar influence can come from the overall environmental energy pattern represented in Figure 7 as the shaded area. The combination of the thoughts, feelings and emotions of all the people in an area, along with the energy of the location itself, are what make up this psychic influence. Its potential for affecting you is obvious. It is an energy pattern that constantly and totally surrounds you. Think back to how you have felt in different locations. Contrast the difference in feeling between a crowded city street and a country area, or compare the difference in vibration between a wedding chapel and a funeral home or hospital. If you do not know how to discern, screen and protect yourself, the vibration of a harsh, negative or densely populated environment can have a noticeable impact upon you. Thinking you can avoid (without precautions) this form of psychic pollution is like thinking you can immerse yourself in a bathtub of dirty water and be able to come away clean.

The final type of environmental influence illustrated in Figure 7 is that of souls in confusion, souls that have passed on but remain attached to Earth or to a specific area. Represented by the circles to the left, they are also thought of as ghosts and poltergeists or just the remaining negative energy of confused people who have passed away. They are usually only confused souls that for one reason or another grew overly attached to aspects of physical life on Earth (food, drink, possessions, a loved one, physical pleasures) and do not want to or are afraid to leave. To the extent that you have some of the same fears or areas of confusion, you can attract them to you like a magnet and thus be affected further by their negative energies and confused vibrations.

Each of these three environmental influences is a reality of the world we live in. By themselves they are not overly menacing or dangerous. In combination with a lack of psychic protection, however, they can have a strong influence on your life. If you are unaware of these types of psychic pollution, you are usually unprotected against them. This makes you even more susceptible to their pressures and influences.

The number of people walking around feeling upset, depressed or anxious because they are picking up the depression of others and do not realize it, or because they are being adversely affected by a negative environment, is enormous. Think about it. How many times have you been nervous, anxious or depressed and could not pinpoint exactly why? Have you ever had a feeling of distress or depression envelop you without any specific events to trigger it? If so, you have experienced the effects of psychic pollution. The sensitivities you did not know you had may have been working against you rather than for you.

The Key Is to Learn by Doing

All of this begins to paint a rather bleak picture: a soul trapped into thinking of itself as only a limited physical body, then maneuvered and controlled by conditioned habit patterns and a lack of set awareness, and finally negatively pressured and affected by polluting environmental psychic influences. What can you do to remedy this situation?

Whether you train with a teacher or pursue independent studies, the key is to learn by doing. Through a consistent step-by-step process, you can leave behind your old limitations and mental shackles.

*Figure 8: Learning to be a soul that has a body
and exploring the unlimited capabilities of the soul*

First, as illustrated in Figure 8, pursue living the statement, "You are a soul that has a body." Explore methods for fully feeling and understanding your real self, your soul nature. As you increase your soul consciousness, the fact that you are a soul that has a body becomes an unshakable reality for you.

Further, as illustrated in the second half of Figure 7, explore the unlimited freedoms of soul-awareness, soul-blending and soul-travel that are the birthright of a Free Soul.

Second, get to know yourself, to vastly increase your levels of selfawareness and self-understanding. It is hard to become a master of the seas of life if you do not know the captain of your own ship yourself. Study material devoted to improving your self-acceptance, self-worth and self-image. Learning goal-setting, direction in life and ways of reducing inner negativity and depression are also essential.

Third, learn to identify the symptoms and effects of conditioning mechanisms. This knowledge provides the beginning tools with which you can break the limiting and controlling effects of programming. By identifying the various forms of conditioning surrounding you, at least half of their influence is broken.

This knowledge, combined with the increased self-understanding gained from your other areas of study, lead to the process illustrated in Figure 9. Gradually, as you gain greater self-mastery, you will learn to break the controlling influence of conditioned habit patterns. You

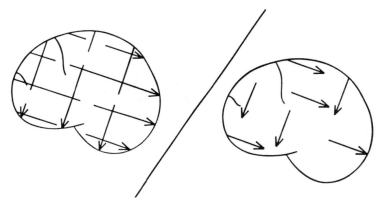

Figure 9: Breaking programmed habit patterns
and eliminating unwanted conditionings

then begin to sort out what programming is useful to you and what is harmful or limiting. At that point you can consciously decide to keep what is beneficial and get rid of what controls and restricts your personal and spiritual freedom.

You can continue the process one step further by learning to program yourself to achieve the goals, qualities and directions that you want out of life. You will eventually learn to program yourself for unlimitedness. These skills, added to those of tapping the soul and its unlimited potentials, bring you two-thirds of the way home to being a fully Free Soul.

The final part of that journey is illustrated in Figure 10, learning to be a master of your own environment. As you learn techniques that teach how to cleanse, solidify and control your aura, you will be better able to protect yourself against psychic pollution. You will learn to screen out the disruptive influences in your environment that come from other people's thoughts and feelings or from souls in confusion.

Further, by learning to utilize fully the perceptions of psychic audience, feeling, vision and prophecy (intuition), you vastly increase your awareness of psychic energy around you. This extra awareness, coupled with the added protection of aura control, make you less vulnerable to the effects and influences of outside pressures in your environment.

These skills provide the defensive half of learning to become a master of your environment and destiny. The second half, that of

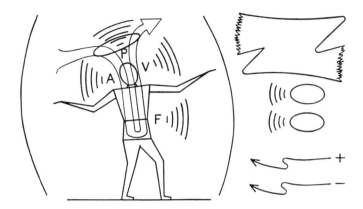

Figure 10: Control of your environment, energy and sensitivities

learning to direct and build your own life's goals, is also aided as you learn greater psychic awareness and energy control. Cleansing techniques teach you how to increase the spiritual energy flow through your body. Biofeedback and inner-vision techniques introduce you to revolutionary methods for stress reduction and self-healing. The increased psychic awareness you can develop also makes it easier to create the opportunities and circumstances needed to complete your goals. With methods for solid protection against outside influences and increased capabilities for sensitivity, health and energy control, you truly become a master of your own destiny and complete the third phase of learning to be a Free Soul. Most important, you will learn to become your own teacher.

Here is quick proof that you can, right now, enter a new realm, that of sensing the spiritual energies that exist around you. Pause a moment here to feel for yourself the energy that radiates from the body and the aura. Get several people to join you for this brief, informal technique. Bring your hands slowly down over the hands of another person until your hands are about three to four inches above theirs. Notice how you can sense an energy interaction or boundary at that point. Many people describe it as a sensation of pushing on foam rubber or of the air feeling denser. Some people feel a warmth, a coolness or a tingling. What is important at this point is not what you feel with the first person, but how you will notice that different

You Have a Team
of Spiritual Helpers
to Travel with You

Figure 11: Your personal team of spiritual guides

people's aura boundaries feel different (some warm, some cool, some thicker and so on). This difference is proof that what you are feeling is real and that you can, with very little training, begin to sense the energies around you with greater awareness.

If you cannot readily get two or three people to join your experiment with this mini-technique, at least bring your own hands together from a distance and feel your own aura boundary.

As tremendous as is everything discussed thus far, there is still more. The greatest blessing of all is the realization that you do not travel alone in your learning journey through life.

As illustrated in Figure 11, each of us has a team of spiritual helpers who travel with us and provide aid, assistance and guidance as we go through life. These spirit guides are souls who have mastered the areas of physical life that you have chosen or need to work on. Various faiths and religions call them by different names ranging from guides, teachers and masters to angels and guardian angels. Whatever you call them, they are your team of spiritual helpers whose primary purpose is to assist you, as a fellow Free Soul, through the lessons and challenges of life.

Most people have between two and eight spirit guides to work with them in a lifetime. How many you have is not necessarily an indication of how spiritual (or conversely, how incapable) you are, but rather is based on the range and variety of wisdom you will require to achieve the goals you have set for yourself in this life.

These highly evolved souls have been with you since birth. They are in many ways the best friends you will ever have because they love, support and care for you unconditionally. They freely share their wisdom and experience, whether or not you follow their guidance.

Many people experience that loving, helping hand in dreams, as warning feelings or as ideas that come to them out of the blue in their moments of greatest need. Your guides are constantly trying to communicate with you. Most often the block in communication is due to your not being attuned to their frequency. The more you open your psychic senses, the easier it is for them to reach you.

Your guides can also reach you through a trance-medium (a channeler). Several of the subsequent articles in this book are submitted by trance-mediums bringing through the words and thoughts of channeled entities.

But it is possible for you to learn to self-channel. That way you always have the freedom to communicate directly with your own guides, anywhere and at any time.

Pursue all of these areas (psychic sensitivity, self-understanding, programming elimination, mastery of your environment and communication with your guides) and the result is freedom. You will become a spiritual free agent, a Free Soul with the tools and methods to grow spiritually in your own unique way. You will be capable of exploring to the fullest your relationship with yourself, with the universe and with God, in the manner that is right for you.

Take the initiative: learn to live the unlimited potentials that are your birthright as a Free Soul!

Recommended Reading

I have always felt that all great spiritual truths are essentially clear, straightforward and simple, so the books recommended as additional reading all have those truths interwoven into the fabric of their simplicity. They are:

Bach, Richard. *Illusions.* New York: Delacorte, 1977.

Bach, Richard. *Jonathan Livingston Seagull.* New York: Avon, 1976.

Gibran, Kahlil. *The Prophet.* New York: Random, 1985.

Heinlein, Robert. *Stranger in a Strange Land*. New York: Ace Books, 1987.

Hesse, Herman. *Siddhartha*. New York: Bantam, 1982.

Moses, Jeffrey. *Oneness: Great Principles Shared by All Religions*. New York: Fawcett, 1989.

Tannen, Deborah. *You Just Don't Understand — Women and Men In Conversation*. New York: Morrow, 1990.

2

Reincarnation: Fact or Fantasy?

Patricia-Rochelle Diegel, Ph.D.

Four-fifths of the world's population believe in reincarnation, or past lives. Why is it that the so-called advanced civilizations have put this concept on the back burner? Some church groups have gone so far as to remove writings that refer to reincarnation from original Biblical writings, Bibles and publications.

However, when one is ready for a quantum leap in consciousness, one can start by reading books on reincarnation. The next thing is to find a reputable consultant who does past-life readings. Then one can find a reputable past-life regressionist who can take one back into past lives to provide final, personal proof.

There is, perhaps, no philosophical doctrine that has the intellectual ancestry of reincarnation, the unfolding of the human spirit or soul through recurring lives on Planet Earth. Reincarnation is taught and illustrated throughout Hindu literature. Buddha also taught it and spoke of his own past births. Pythagoras did the same, and Plato included it in his writings. Josephus said it was accepted among the Hebrews.

Solomon said being born with a perfect body was the reward for having been good in prior lives. Jesus told his disciples that John the Baptist had been Elijah. Virgil and Ovid took it for granted. Egyptians created rituals in their temples to show they believed we return to a new body. Origen, a very learned Christian father, said that everyone received a body based upon his or her actions in a former life. In the Middle Ages, a learned person of Islam said, "I died out of stone and I became a plant; I died out of the plant and I became an animal; I died out of the animal and I became a man. Why, then,

should I fear death? When I finish my lives as a man then I shall die
and I shall become an angel."

Past lives were sung of in Norse legends, which taught that many
lives had to be lived in order to enter Valhalla. Plato and other Greek
as well as Roman philosophers believed in reincarnation. Indians of
many tribes including Sioux, Zuni, Aztec, Inca and Hopi have tales of
their priests and chiefs returning in new bodies.

Goethe, in his old age, looked forward joyfully to his return; Hume
said that reincarnation was the only doctrine of immortality that a
philosopher could look at and totally believe. It was a view shared by
British professor Taggart, who, in reviewing the various theories of
immortality, came to the conclusion that reincarnation was the most
rational philosophy. Great literary giants also believed in it:
Wordsworth, Rossetti, Browning and many others. Some people say
that the coming into existence of a soul depends on the formation of
a body and that the soul will disappear when the body dies. How
could a soul with no past and a short life have an "everlasting future?"
Reincarnation.

The Akashic Records

The Akashic Records hold the experiences of all the lives humankind has lived. Some psychics say that the Akashic Records are stored
in books. Now that the human race has been introduced to photo-
graphs and movies, other psychics who read past lives see the Akashic
Records on "film." The more evolved psychic sees the past lives of
others in three dimensions – a hologram – and quite often finds
himself or herself in the scene. The very advanced Akashic reader
can be in the scene and turn around to see the client and everything
else present.

The concept of reincarnation restores justice to God and power to
human beings. Every human spirit enters into incarnating without
knowledge, without conscience, without discrimination. By experience, both pleasant and painful, we create materials and build them
into mental and moral faculties. Thus, the character we are born with
is self-made and marks the stage we have reached in the long process
of evolution, life after life. The good disposition and the fine capacities of a noble nature are the gifts of many hard-fought lives. The
savage of today is the saint of the future. We all walk a similar road;

we all are destined for ultimate human perfection.

In reincarnation the "master key" is found: consciousness needs a brain in order to express itself on the physical plane just as a musician needs an instrument. Consciousness exists before conception, so we choose the parents we'll have and sometimes we even get those two people together so we'll have the correct genetic line (sometimes known as one-night stands). We need those genetic lines to accomplish the goals we have chosen for that upcoming life. Also, we know ahead of time whether we will stay with those parents or will be adopted by other parents in order to fulfill our goals and purposes.

Our ego/soul unfolds its powers through evolving itself in many successive incarnations on other planets or on the Earth plane. But sometimes an ego/soul will wait a few hundred years before it returns to a body, working on the "other side of life" as a guide for those in bodies in order to earn "evolutionary points." As the ego/soul gains more positive experiences, its incarnations occur closer together, sometimes even twice in the same century, in improved bodies and better situations until it has passed all the tests the Earth plane has to offer. When this has been accomplished, the ego/soul graduates.

Liberated from the wheel of birth and death after reaching a certain level of awareness, it then has a choice of continuing its evolution on higher planes or on other planets. The ego/soul can elect to stay on Planet Earth, either in human form as a master teacher or in spiritual form as a master in the hierarchy of this planet, in order to be of service to the human race.

Evolution Through the Kingdoms

The cycle of birth and death and rebirth is only a part of the great process of human evolution. We have found that all other life forms also evolve, first within their own kingdoms, then eventually moving up to the next higher level of life forms.

At the bottom of the scale is the mineral kingdom — rocks, gems and crystals, plus manufactured items made from minerals, vegetables or animals that are no longer alive. Then comes the self-reproducing, invisible kingdom of microbes, bacteria, viruses and so on, all things that procreate themselves but do not have parents.

The next level is the vegetable kingdom: plants, trees and so on, and that which they give life to such as fruit, flowers and vegetables.

They have male and female energies in order to reproduce.

The next level is the lower animal kingdom, from insects to dinosaurs, those who have parents (a male and a female) in order to reproduce.

The next level is the middle animal kingdom such as trainable animals in circuses and zoos and those used in sports such as racing and hunting. They have parents (a male and a female) and are given a name by their owners.

The next level is the higher animal kingdom. These are the pets of humans. They are usually given more than one name and therefore they evolve faster. If they are given a first name that relates to their conscious mind, they answer to it and obey their mistress or master (most of the time). The last name should be the same as that of their owner because that connects them to the subconscious mind of the owner. They become very telepathic with that owner as well as with those humans or other animals who live in the same space. If they are given a middle name, then they have a connection to the higher levels of awareness through the superconscious mind of the planet and those around them and they evolve more rapidly into the human kingdoms.

The next level is the animal-human kingdom, the aborigine who is still part of a group soul and has the powers of telepathy and teleportation. More advanced humans have lost the memory of how to do these things.

The next level is the human-animal kingdom which encompasses the majority of people on this planet, the masses who do not have a real conscience. This is why we still have wars and crime. Some of them can be very intellectual but do not understand the laws of evolution and have not yet been awakened, so they are limited in many ways.

The next level is the human kingdom, or those people with a real conscience and a desire to do something for the rest of the human race, as well as for the lower kingdoms. Also at this level people begin to use more of their potential — artistic and creative talents, as well as psychic and intuitive abilities.

The people in the human kingdom can do a great deal to help others in the animal-human and human-animal groups by becoming their teachers, counselors, mentors and friends.

The Higher Levels of the Advanced Human Kingdom

Awareness:

Metaphysicians: These people are balancers and healers and they do their healings using prana energy (ki or chi); they are beyond the ordinary healers.

Magicians: These people make things happen; their powers are from higher sources and they work for the good of all.

Metaphysicists: These people pull information from beyond the third dimension and can do things ordinary scientists cannot even comprehend.

Beingness:

Mystics: These people have insights from higher levels of consciousness and higher spiritual realms.

Occultists: These people are very aware and use true alchemy and higher knowledge to help humankind.

True Gurus: These people share what they know with others and then release their followers to go and teach so the knowledge is passed on to all those who are ready to learn and then to act and share.

Catalysts: These people affect others with their higher energies and their insights into spiritual truths.

Knowingness:

Planetary Adepts: These people are the knowers of truth.

World Teachers: These people create religions or philosophies based upon universal truths.

World Leaders: These people carry on the religions, traditions and teachings of the world teachers, sharing their higher vibrations with others on the path.

World Servers: These people are also very evolved, but they work behind the scenes with very special people and do not let others know who they are or what their missions are all about.

Free Beings: These people move from group to group, sharing the truths taught by world teachers and leaders.

Oneness:

Master Teachers: These people live in invisible mansions on empty lots. When the public is ready, the master teacher makes contact telepathically or in person and then prepares the pupil for his or her true role in the current life.

Masters: These people are members of the planetary hierarchy who do not have to come back into a human body unless they choose to in order to help the human race evolve more rapidly or to help avert a major problem that can't be solved without their assistance.

We All Have the Right to Know Who We Were in Past Lives

Aside from karma, the subjects most asked about when people discuss reincarnation are déjà vu, soulmates and counterparts. We need to understand more about conscious evolution — that everyone has had past lives as a non-Earthling or an Earthling or both.

Déjà vu: traveling physically to faraway places and distant memories in order to call forth positive talents, knowledge and abilities from past lives into this brain and this body and to magnetize people from past lives who can enhance the present life; reexperiencing our most positive, creative, spiritual and/or interesting past lives physically, emotionally and mentally, or to clear up negative past-life karma.

Soulmates: finding out who the important people in our present life were to us in other lifetimes, what type of relationship we had with them and where those lives took place. There are three categories:

> *Blood Relatives:* ancestors, grandparents, parents, brothers and sisters, aunts, uncles and cousins, children, grandchildren, nieces and nephews and so on.

> *Love Relationships:* spouses, lovers, mistresses, owners, slaves and so on.

> *Coworkers:* bosses, employees, equals, miscellaneous contacts and so on.

The strength of these ties depends on how deeply involved we were with the person in other lives. Unrequited love or sudden loss creates "aka threads" that pull us back into each other's future incarnations.

Counterparts: finding out who in our present life shares with us a common origin, either non-Earthly or Earthly; such people seem to be pulled to each other more quickly.

> *Non-Earthlings:*
>> those from the current universe
>> those from the same galaxy
>> those from the same constellation

those from the same solar system
those from the same planet
those from the same original race on that planet
Earthlings:
those from the Planet Earth.
those who have evolved up from the mineral kingdom
those who have evolved up from the plant/elemental kingdom
those who have evolved up from the animal kingdom
those who have come through the animal-human kingdom
  (the aborigines); these can be non-Earthling or Earthling
those who have come through the human-animal kingdom
  (the masses); these can be non-Earthling or Earthling.
Both groups eventually move into the human kingdom.

Present-life Karma and Past-life Karma

Karma reflects the old saying, "As ye sow so shall ye reap."
Karma is the law of cause and effect.

Individual karma: thoughts, actions and emotions reaped directly from another lifetime. They can be either positive or negative. These are sins of omission, things we didn't do that we should have done, and sins of commission, things we did that we shouldn't have done.

Family karma: returning to people again and again to complete unfinished projects, commitments and promises. Sometimes we change roles to fulfill our purposes because we need to be in that gender or the role we need to play needs that type of body. Sometimes the ego/soul will travel halfway around the world to complete karmic patterns.

Collective group karma: churches, organizations, lodges, companies, schools, political parties and so forth. When we spend a lot of time with one group in a particular lifetime we frequently come back as part of that group. We can finish up things left unfinished in the prior life or add something new to the group.

National karma: being a part of the growth of a nation will bring us back in a future life to continue that positive growth. If negative actions have been taken by that nation, we may choose to go back to help clear up the national karma. Wars, revolutions, the fall of empires, enslavement of others and so forth are examples of this kind of karma.

Racial karma: we share both positive and negative karmas created by any race that we have been part of, even if the action didn't occur while we were in that race. We may come back into that race to help release the negative karmas and enhance the positive ones. The more evolved we are, the more likely we are to move into a race for that reason.

Try, Try Again

We are all masters of our tomorrows, however much we are hampered today by the results of our yesterdays.

Karmic force works itself out on the plane on which it was generated. Thought works on the mental plane, builds character and adds to knowledge. Desire works on the astral/emotional plane. Opportunities for good will develop into more opportunities for good. Good can overcome evil. Action works on the physical plane and builds better environmental conditions.

It is time to neutralize our negative karma and begin to eradicate our subconscious problems. Many of them have their origins in our past lives. It is important that we locate them and start our journey up the spiritual path to enlightenment.

The universe is a one-piece whole. Every atom and vibration, every unit of life force in manifestation on the physical, emotional, mental, creative or spiritual plane (whether human, animal, vegetable, mineral or etheric) acts on and reacts to every other unit. We are interrelated because we are a part of the universe and we are also the total universe in action.

If we would let the truth of reincarnation sink deep into our hearts, we could no longer envy others for the qualities they possess or lament our own limitations. Envy and limitation alike arise from ignorance of the law by means of which those powers we admire may be made our own. It is not by foolish envy or idle dreaming we achieve those powers, but by making the effort to develop them within ourselves. Then there is no goal so high we cannot reach it. Persistent effort is required, and many lives may be needed for the winning. There is no real failure in life except the lack of courage to try again after each apparent failure.

Time Tracking

Can we get off the wheel of reincarnation? Yes. How can we do it? There are specific techniques we can use to scan our own past lives in order to bring forth all of our talents, knowledge and abilities from positive past lives. We can also clear up all of our negative karma from limited past lives. Understanding reincarnation, its place and its purpose for mankind on the probationary path, will set us free. We do not go back into animal bodies but must move forward on the evolutionary path from savage, primitive, underprivileged, low-skilled beings to highly skilled thinkers, knowers, artists, psychics, balancers, healers, energizers, consultants, transformers, teachers, leaders, advanced souls and so on. We can accomplish several of these levels in one lifetime if we have released old karmic blocks and patterns that can hold us back. We can evolve very rapidly if we are willing to utilize the best from our present-life training and access the best from our past lives. Then we will be able to create our own future lives and live them while we are still in our current bodies.

What brings us back time after time?

Phase one is the young soul reincarnating, thirsting for experience: love, beauty, talents, success, power, desire for more knowledge about everything, including a desire to clear up negative karma and then to help others clear up theirs.

Phase two is the evolving soul reincarnating, developing our own inherent powers and knowing that God lives equally in all of us as we evolve. We locate our positive karma from past lives and are able to utilize it again.

Phase three is the mature soul leaving the reincarnating cycle. We help others to evolve and learn to use our inherent powers. We accept physical embodiment as a gift to be used for spiritual growth.

When the form is pure and the inner God shines forth, we will be able to leave the wheel of incarnations and move to the higher realms of Light!

Recommended Reading

Diegel, Patricia-Rochelle. *Last Stop to Infinity* (Available in the Fall of 1993.)

Diegel, Patricia-Rochelle and Jon-Terrance. *Past Lives of the Rich and (In)Famous.* (Available in the Spring of 1994.)

Fiore, Edith. *You Have Been Here Before.* New York: Ballatine, 1986.

Goldberg, Bruce. *Past Lives/Future Lives.* New York: Ballatine, 1988.

Hall, Manley Palmer. *Reincarnation: the Cycle of Necessity.* Los Angeles: Philosophical Research, 1978.

Head, Joseph and Cranston, S.L. *Reincarnation: The Phoenix Fire Mystery.* San Diego: Point Loma Publishing, 1991.

MacLaine, Shirley. *Dancing in the Light.* New York: Bantam, 1985.

Steiner, Rudolph. *Reincarnation and Immortality.* Blauvelt, N.Y.: Garber Communications, 1970.

3

The Chakras

Hallie Deering

The cerebrospinal centers that channel energy from the higher planes into the physical form resemble whirlpools of incoming Light/energy. Therefore, they are called "chakras," from the Sanskrit word for wheels. We count seven or sometimes eight major chakras — some people count thirteen — but there are also hundreds of minor chakras all over the surface of the body, which we know as the acupuncture points. These minor chakras are formed by criss-crosses in the energy lines emanating from the major chakras. These lines of energy that link the minor chakras are called "meridians." As you might have already guessed from the description, this vast system of chakras and meridians corresponds very nicely with the Earth's vast network of vortices and ley lines. The terminology is different, but the appearance and function of the energy flow are similar

States of healing as well as deep states of superconsciousness, are achieved by working through the chakra system in order to access the subtle bodies. Authorities differ as to the exact number, location and color scheme of the chakras. This is due primarily to different body types and the degree and direction of each individual soul's evolution. For example, there is much controversy over whether the third chakra is located at the navel or the solar plexus. Both locations are correct: people who have incarnated extensively in our Western civilizations will tend to focus energy in the navel chakra, while individuals who have incarnated time after time in Eastern civilizations will focus energy in the solar plexus. When in doubt, balance both chakras.

The chakra system presented here is simple and effective for everyone since it includes both navel and solar plexus chakras. We will discuss thirteen chakras which run in a fairly straight line from the groin up to the top of the head and somewhat beyond.

Seen from the side view of the body, the chakras look like whirling funnels of colored Light. The narrow ends of the funnels are attached to the spinal column; they pass from the back of the body through to the front and widen out several inches beyond the front of the body.

Seen from the front of the body, the chakras look like flowers with opened petals or like ornate wheels with many spokes. These effects are due to the energy that radiates out from the center of each chakra. The number of petals or spokes that manifest depends on the frequency of the energy flowing through each center. The lower frequency of the base chakra manifests only four petals, while the much higher frequency of the crown chakra manifests a thousand petals of cascading Light.

Because the spinal energies raise their frequency as they flow upward, there is also a rainbow effect to the colors of the chakra system, ranging from infrared at the groin to ultraviolet and bright gold around the top of the head.

All in all, the living Light of the chakra system is a beautiful sight to behold as it pulsates with brilliantly hued energy flowing in from all the different planes of creation. Normally, this energy field (the physical aura) spreads out to a distance of about eighteen inches from the physical body. When a person begins to evolve spiritually, pulling more and more high-frequency energy down from the finer planes into the physical body, the colors of the chakras purify into a dazzling resplendency that defies description as the auric field grows larger and larger. The masters say the Buddha's aura had a radius of three miles!

It is well worth our while to take a brief look at each center separately, because if you understand your chakras you will better understand yourself.

The first, or base, chakra grounds your soul's energy onto the physical plane. This chakra opens in the lower pubic region whence it connects back to the tip of the spine (the coccyx). It vibrates at the deep red end of the spectrum, sometimes displaying a violet tinge. For men this is the sexual center. The first chakra stores stress and pollution;

when its energy is balanced, tension is released and past-life talents begin to reappear. A well-tuned base chakra leads to emotional stability and a feeling of being centered and grounded. The colors red and black open and ground this Earth-oriented chakra. When the first chakra is overactive (as in the case of sexual obsession), green closes it.

The second chakra is midway between the first chakra and the navel. This center is a beautiful, vibrant orange color. Closely connected with creativity and motherhood, this is the sexual center for women. Stress, anger and sexual repression result when this chakra is out of adjustment. Balancing the second chakra leads to increased creativity, integrated emotions and greater success in intimate relationships. Orange opens this center; blue closes it.

The navel center works in conjunction with the solar plexus and displays a bright yellow glow. Psychosomatic and emotional problems, grief, depression and stress can result from an imbalance of this energy. A balanced navel chakra heightens sensitivity and intuition. Yellow opens the navel center; violet closes it.

The solar plexus chakra is as bright as the noonday sun. It shines with a brilliant golden-white Light. This complex chakra is the juncture of the lower chakras — the Earth-oriented centers — and the upper, spiritual centers. The astral body connects to the physical body through the solar plexus chakra. The astral vehicle is sometimes referred to as the emotional body because it is the seat of our emotions. This is why inner turmoil causes a tight feeling in the region of the solar plexus, as negative emotions flow through that chakra directly into the astral body, resulting in tension at the connecting point. If you wish to clear emotional problems, this is the chakra on which to focus. Trauma from past lives and old karma also leave their residue in the solar plexus energy, and this often must be dissipated before progress is possible on higher levels. A harmonious solar plexus brings emotional serenity, physical well-being and an increasing ability to use the astral body during sleep. White and gold open the solar plexus; since white Light is composed of all the colors, no color closes it. Black tends to ground the astral energies back down into the physical body.

The heart chakra's color is green, although a happy, mellow heart chakra throws out every color of the rainbow in clear, delicate shades. Imbalance in the heart energy leads to circulatory problems, deficiencies of the immune system and emotional extremes. This is the major balancing center for the subtle bodies; just as the physical heart pumps blood to all parts of the body, so the heart chakra pulsates energy throughout the auric field. In addition, the astral body has a strong influence on the heart center, as does the soul itself. An open, loving, divinely connected heart chakra such as that of Christ looks like a constantly changing kaleidoscope of complex geometric patterns and exquisite colors. Many pure colors open the heart; green is the primary color, but gold, rose and violet are also highly desirable.

The throat chakra is light blue in color. This chakra controls astral hearing (clairaudience) and many nonvisual types of channeling, as well as the ability to express oneself clearly and effectively. Problems with the throat energy impact the speech centers and the immune system, while the inability to express oneself can lead to illness resulting from suppressed emotions. Light blue opens the throat; orange closes it.

The third-eye chakra is so well-known that it even appears on the one-dollar bills of the United States, and just about every culture has knowledge of it. Actually, there are two third-eye centers, one low on the forehead and one higher up. It is both of these centers working together that gives your inner vision clarity and depth, just as your two physical eyes working together gives physical depth perception. The energy of the lower third-eye center vibrates at a deep cobalt blue frequency; the higher third-eye center manifests indigo blue. An imbalance in either center causes hallucinations and an inability to distinguish fantasy from reality. Balanced third-eye centers, however, bring valuable gifts: intuitive understanding, spiritual inspiration, the ability to visualize clearly and visions of the finer planes. With an opened third eye one begins to see the nature of the divine. The mental body connects to the physical brain through the upper and lower third-eye centers, so it is through these chakras that access is gained to the fifth dimension. Cobalt blue and indigo open the third-eye centers; red and yellow close them.

The crown chakra has as its colors violet and lavender. It is through this vital center that divine forces nourish the physical being. Because of the divine energy flow, there is no negativity associated with the crown chakra. Through the soft skin over the crown, the spirit enters the body of a child in the womb; usually through this same doorway the life force retreats upon the death of the physical body. A fully opened crown chakra radiates divine Light in the thousand-petaled lotus shape referred to in the Eastern scriptures. When this center is balanced, connection with the divine is tangible. Violet and lavender open the crown; no color closes it.

The five chakras above the crown are nonphysical centers that connect with the highest subtle bodies. We will not deal with them in detail, as it will suffice to say that pink, silver and deep gold are the essential colors here, and there are also other colors that go beyond the physical spectrum. The gold nimbus seen in portraits of Christ and the great masters refers to this energy.

Your Doorways to Limitless, Multidimensional Possibilities

Because the energy of each chakra maintains the body organs that are located in its vicinity, a chakra system that is properly cleaned, balanced and aligned is a ticket to improved physical well-being. Because the chakras connect to the subtle bodies, they are also windows that look out on glorious, divine landscapes. Through these windows you can explore other times, other places, other worlds, other dimensions and other forms of being. Through them also you can contact the divine mind and the holy masters, which is the beginning of deep spiritual fulfillment.

Down through the chakra system sweeps the multidimensional energy that sustains the physical body; up through the chakra system flows the information gathered from this plane on its way to the soul itself. Needless to say, it behooves us all to keep this vital energy network functioning as perfectly as possible.

Recommended Reading

Choa Kok Sui. *Chronic Healing.* Makati, Metro Manila: Institute for Inner Studies, 1989.

Gurudas. *Gem Elixirs and Vibrational Healing,* Volume 1. Boulder, Colorado: Cassandra Press, 1985. Information channeled by Kevin Reyerson.

Leadbeater, C. W. *The Chakras.* Wheaton, IL: The Theosophical Publishing House, 1980.

4

What Is Channeling?

Vywamus through Barbara Burns

Greetings, my dear friends.

Many people ask me, "Vywamus, what is channeling and why should I get involved with it?" Sometimes they also ask me, "Why are you teachers so interested in channeling? You never used to be. It seems to us you never really came to us before about this, at least not that we can remember." Well, you know, I think these are very good questions. I really appreciate the opportunity to answer them.

What is channeling? I think it is really very simple. In many ways, being a channel is like being an electrical transformer, those pieces of equipment you use to take one level of energy and step it up or down to another level of energy that is operating at a different vibrational frequency. You see, the great Plan of the Source as it relates to physicality involves many levels or dimensions of consciousness, wherein beings, similar to you and different, have their experiencing. As you are aware, the evolutionary Plan of the Source also involves movement from level to level, upward ever more expansively. The energy from the Creative Core of the Source flows from level to level. Now, how do you suppose it gets from one level to the other? It is not simply poured out without order or focus. No. You see, everything within the Divine Plan, the whole structure, is based upon consciousness, consciousness serving the Plan and the Light. The expressed energy, the Light of the Source, flows outward from the Creative Core by means of consciousness. All of us, as channels, help step that energy level down from one level to the next.

You see I, Vywamus, am a channel, and that is really one of the main things I do. My soul's purposes or my self's purposes are very involved in consciously transmitting energy from higher frequencies. I bring it right through my own being and I step it down to a vibrational rate that is perhaps a little slower. When I am working with you and you are truly opening up to your greater consciousness in a more cosmic way, I am able to bring to you knowledge, information, energy, love and Light from levels in which you are not yet consciously focused. Through my channeling these energies can come to you stepped down into an frequency that is more comfortable for you.

You see, as channels, you are all stepping the energy down from the highest level that you can reach right into the Earth, and that is one of the most important reasons why you are in physicality. You are channeling from the soul level, the spiritual plane, into the Earth where the Earth needs it to advance her evolutionary purposes and those of humanity.

Now, of course, everybody is a channel. You know quite well that, as a personality level expression, you are a creation of your soul. The way your soul has done this is by extending itself into physicality and channeling its life force into you. To do this it must step down its energy to a lower vibrational rate in order that you are able to integrate fully into the vibrational level of the Earth plane and thereby live comfortably in it. Channeling in one sense, then, is just bringing the life force from one level to another by means of your own energy format. You are doing it all the time while you are living and breathing here upon the planet. In that sense, everyone is a channel.

However, if you want to become a channel in a more conscious way, working and focusing in a more purposeful fashion, that is really what I, Vywamus, am here to assist you with. The focus now of our work is channeling from the spiritual plane, where your souls and the spiritual teachers who are assisting the Earth's growth now function for the most part. From this level the divine love and Light are brought down into physicality where humanity needs it. That is what I think channeling is.

Now this means that what you are dealing with when you are channeling is transmitting energy in a pure form. You can decide how you are going to utilize it. In what specialized ways are you going to channel this energy? Many people do this in the form of art, music and dance and that is a wondrous way of channeling. I really love channeling pure sound, for sound is so powerful and so moving. That is one of the reasons that I love voice channeling because the voice makes sounds. It is also a way that you can express the energy so that others can share it.

Now, of course, you know about channeling healing energy to assist yourselves and others to heal, balance and align their bodies. So you see, it is just really a question of how you decide to express or utilize the energy that you are transforming from one level to another.

As I have said, I am particularly fond of voice channeling because I love the effect that sound has. Sound is a very powerful creative element and it doesn't matter if you just bring it through by toning. That is a wondrous way of expressing energy and that is surely voice channeling, wouldn't you agree with me? However, sometimes it is very, very helpful to channel in a conceptual way and, of course, this requires the use of concepts and words to bring in the essence of an idea from the spiritual plane, conveying it in a coherent package of words and sentences that you can express with your voice to other people so that they can understand it.

How is that done? Well, I would say it is really very simple. You see, when you were a little child, you did not have any words at first, not that you could remember anyway. What you saw was a world full of shapes and colors and different kinds of energy. One of the very first energies you were able to recognize and put a word to was the energy of your mother. You found a word with the help of others that best expressed your sense of this energy and you also found words for the energy of your father and for colors and shapes and all kinds of other things. You even found words for things that you could not see, such as heat and cold and happiness. You learned to find words for ideas, things, people and also for feelings and sensations. As you traveled through your life, you gathered a wonderful collection of words to describe all kinds of experiencing and this word-assigning activity is a part of what your mental body does for you.

These words and concepts are available in your mental body and, as you grow up, you no longer have to think about what word matches a particular color or shape. Right away the word "table" springs to mind when you see a table. You don't have to ask yourself to call up

the word for table. When you see the color red you don't have to stop
and say, "Yes a color, well, um, all right now mental body, give me the
word for that particular color. Oh, red. Oh yes, thank you." You
don't really do that, do you? No. It is very fast, very automatic and
that is why voice channels who are somewhat experienced in using
this talent for channeling can talk very flowingly and easily. They
very effortlessly translate energy into words without having to think
any more about it than you do when you see the color red and say,
"That is red." You see? It is not very hard at all. It is really just
giving yourself permission and giving the soul or spiritual teachers
permission to use these skills that you have acquired.

Sometimes I think we should rename the process "word channeling" because it doesn't really matter for your own purposes if you
translate the energy into words inside your heart and head without
speaking and just hear them yourself. That is a wonderful way to have
a moment-to-moment discussion with your soul and spiritual teachers.
It helps you to bring their support and guidance right into your daily
life. Sometimes, however, you want to share with others all the
wonderful things that are coming through. You use the same word
faculty that you have been using within your mind and heart, but this
time you have to use the throat and voice to project it outward. It is
not very different at all.

Now, I have often used the word "translate" when I speak about
channeling and I would like to pause and consider that with you for a
moment. In my view, this is what voice channeling is all about. You
see, what you do is you take energy impulses and you turn them into
words. You have heard, I am sure, about the method of communication called "Morse Code." That is the way people used to communicate in your recent past over long distances. Morse Code was really
just energy that was expressed in terms of dots and dashes, or quick
pulses and slow pulses. Now to me, that is pretty much the way the
spiritual plane energy comes in through your channel before it's
turned into words, like dots and dashes or energy pulses of different
durations and intensities. If you went to school to learn Morse Code,
what you really would be learning is how to turn those energy pulses
into words. You would learn a language, wouldn't you? It is the
language that allows you to translate energy pulses into words and it is
truly not very difficult.

When learning word channeling, you don't even have to go to school because we are going to facilitate the process within your own minds and hearts, if you are willing. We will convert the energy pulses coming into your mind, heart and throat centers. We are just going to hook them right into that language ability that you learned as a little child. It is really very simple. You can just ask your mental body to allow the connection as you go through the exercise I will make available later in this writing. At first you might have to use your imagination a little, saying, "Well what does that energy feel like? What words seem quite right?" Don't worry. It will come very quickly.

Now the next question that you might ask is, "Why should I be a channel? What good is it to me?" I have already told you that it is a great service to humanity and to the Earth. At this time, many members of humanity cannot connect or believe they cannot connect (which is the same thing) into as high a vibrational frequency as you can when you are in channel. It is easy for you, really it is, to connect with your soul and your spiritual teachers. Through you we can bring in very directly the wonderful Light and love of the Source to the heart of the Earth and to those of humanity who are willing to receive it. With the growth and changes humanity is going through right now, this is greatly needed.

I can tell you that this is one very good reason for you to channel, for it is one of the purposes for which you are here. You came and agreed to have a physical body and one of the reasons you did that is because the Earth needed your assistance in birthing a very unique and wondrous new species, homo sapiens. Of course, you came here to serve your own evolution, but, as in all cases within the Divine Plan, when you serve you are served. Consequently, a benefit for you in the channeling processes is that it helps you to have a very fine connection with the Earth, so that where you are, the Earth is assisted and humanity is more able to grow easily and joyously. I think that this is really an advantage, don't you? It would be nice if your relationship with the Earth and with other humans were more gentle and harmonious, wouldn't it?

How does channeling assist the evolution of self? You did come here to evolve yourselves, you know. You really came because physicality is a training. It is like a schoolhouse that you choose to go to and you must graduate before you can go to the next step. There are many, many things that you need to learn before you take on more cosmic levels of responsibility in assisting the Source to evolve itself through creation.

There is some wonderful training in physicality, indeed. If you are able to talk to your high self, there is a great deal that you can do to enrich your stay in this realm because, you see, the soul knows all the lives that you have lived, all the adventures that you have had, knows the lessons that you have learned and those you might have missed. Your soul has, you might say, and "eagle's-eye" overview of what is happening to you, of your relationships, your choices, your past and your options for the future. Sometimes when you are going through your life, you feel quite blind. It is a little like driving a car when perhaps you don't see well at night, for example. You don't see quite as clearly as you would like to and it gives you a sense of limitation, doesn't it? However, your soul really sees from a higher perspective and is able to appreciate the whole of the path you are traveling on. It can see where you are on the path. It can see where you have come from and, yes friends, it can see the possible destinations that perhaps you cannot see with your physical or mental faculties. Wouldn't it be wonderful to have the soul as your navigator? Wouldn't it be immensely helpful to be able to talk to your soul and find out its perspective? I think you would feel as though you could see everything more clearly and would feel the security and joy of knowing that your choices are really taking you to that which is for your highest and best good as a divine being.

I know that sometimes as you are having your experiences, you get a sense of frustration and a feeling that you have missed the point. There was something there but it passed you by. I think that it is very helpful if you talk to your soul of these things because the soul sees very clearly what opportunities for growth there are in all your adventures and relationships. With its help you can see what truly is there for you. I think that through the soul you have the ability to maximize your opportunities for growth and perhaps to utilize these opportunities in a more joyous way. You know that you can learn a lot by stubbing your toe or banging your head, but you could learn about the same things by being aware of what is there before you experience painful impact. So I think that involving the soul in your daily life will help you to see the points of opportunity for growth and to move into them in a more joyous and easy fashion.

Now that is not to say that everything will be easy just because the soul is involved for, truly, you still have a lot of responsibility for the appropriate action. You see, you can ask your soul about something and your soul can say, "Well, you know, I think that perhaps this opportunity could help us to see such and such, and I think that perhaps our best way of responding to it is to do this and that." However, you have free will. You don't have to listen to anything that the soul says. You can say, "Well, thank you very much, soul. You are not down here and you don't understand at all and I think you should just leave this to me. I am not going to take your advice." Free will operates at every level, truly it does. Sometimes you don't involve the soul as much or you find it rather difficult to stretch yourself to the level that the soul says you are capable of. Always, it is your decision and your responsibility to act in accordance with what you view as the best choice for you. I believe that the channeling process is one of the most powerful and clear ways to get in touch with the soul's ability to assist you with your choices. It is not a process that cuts off your responsibility or your freedom to govern your lives. It simply provides you with a much greater array of tools with which to do so.

There is another helpful aspect to channeling. One of the things I think that you are all asking for is for more support in your lives. I think that many of you feel a little isolated and not very supported sometimes when you are going through your challenges and your growing. Sometimes it feels lonely and painful. Other people seem to have their own problems to concern themselves with and you do not always feel entitled to call upon them. Truly, your friends in physicality are there to support you, and you them, but you also have a beautiful support system available to you on the spiritual plane. It begins with your soul. The Source provided you with the soul level to use as your direct connection into the Divine Creative Core. The Source knew that at times in physicality perhaps this might seem very far away to you. The soul is always there for you, because it *is* you at a more comprehensive level. You know the soul has created this and the other lives you have had in order to learn and evolve its understanding of its own divine nature. At this point in its development, your presence on this physical planet is a very important key to its

next step forward. Therefore, the soul is always ready to pay attention
to you, always there to support you, always loving and grateful toward
you. It brings to you the Light and love of the Source. Don't you
think you could use a little bit of that support in your life?

It is through the soul that you get to link up with the souls of other
people. Yes, you have soul friends, you do. These are friends who
are in body and not in body, whose souls are very dear and close to
your soul, often because of many wonderful adventures you have
shared. These souls are part of your support system and their
personality expressions often are too, if they are on the physical
plane. As well, you link up with us, the spiritual teachers. Isn't that
a wonderful support system? As you begin to more forward in your
evolution, you really want to create your life in a more expansive and
abundant way. The personality-level support systems just don't seem
to be adequate. They don't seem to be comprehensive or strong
enough and they don't perhaps seem to be quite there for you when
you want to really leap forward in your growth. So you need a vaster,
brighter, more connective support system. I think that through
channeling you may be able to make the conscious connections that
will allow you to realize and to utilize, moment-to-moment in a very
practical way in your lives, the wonderful support system that the
Creator put in place for you as part of the Divine Plan.

Now the other question that I believe you might be asking is, "Why
now? Why are the teachers coming to me now talking about channeling? Why did they not come before?" Well, there has been a certain
amount of this kind of channeling on the Earth before. Many of you
who are really drawn to channeling have had earlier training in other
times. Perhaps you began in Atlantis or Lemuria or even before that,
and certainly many of you had really quite sophisticated training in
ancient Egypt. You really don't have to worry about how long it is
going to take you to train in this life. I would say that most of you are
really very ready. You have done all your training, most of it anyway,
in other lives. However, it is true that there is a much greater
emphasis on channeling now. I would say that in the past five to ten
years we have really made a concerted push here on the spiritual
plane. It has only been a few years that I myself have been directly
involved in training channels here upon the Earth. That is because it
is in some ways a bit of an experiment that we on the spiritual plane

decided to try to see if we could assist you, and through you, the Earth and humanity a little more directly than we have been able to do in the past. So you might say that we have recently decided to try to utilize channeling more fully to accomplish our goals of service to the Earth and to aid you in your great service of helping this New Age to come forth on the Earth.

Through the channeling opportunity, we hope to be able to support the Earth and humanity more completely through the present changes so that we may move into all the new beginnings now emerging with flexibility and ease. You have heard quite a bit about how these impending changes are going to be accomplished by a lot of disaster and destruction. Disaster and destruction, from my perspective, really come when one cannot let go of the old without seeing it smashed or broken up. If one is able to let go of the old ways in a very flexible, joyous and adventuresome spirit, it is so much easier to bring in the new without disruption, isn't it? In your own life you have experienced at times that something was no longer appropriate for you. Perhaps it was a relationship, a job or something like that. You really knew that it was coming to an end and that it wasn't serving you very well. Oh, but it was so hard for you to let go, and so you held on and you held on until everything fell apart. Perhaps the relationship blew up quite dramatically or you were fired from the job. Whatever it was just fell apart. That shows you that you can move forward and make changes in a more dramatic and impactful fashion. It's not so bad, because, in the end, the change still comes.

The New Age is going to come, my friends, one way or another, but won't it be wonderful if you are able to let go of the old when it no longer serves you and move into the new with a sense of joy, adventure and confidence? We would like that for all of humanity and for each of you individually as well. I think that channeling is one of the ways that we are going to achieve this. I, myself, have been watching very closely how the channeling has been affecting the growth and change of the Earth and humanity and I can tell you that I am delighted and that I really feel that what perhaps began as an experiment is a full-out success. That is why more and more spiritual teachers are coming more directly to those with whom they communicated in the past in a less direct way. Many of you have been assisting the Divine Plan for the Earth in an unconscious way and it is channeling that can make this a conscious, loving partnership.

Now, many spiritual teachers are really deciding that channeling is the way they want to work with those with whom they are involved on the physical plane. I, myself, am giving lessons here on the spiritual plane to those teachers who are getting excited about the channeling opportunity and how it is really helping them to carry out their service to the Earth in a more direct fashion. Many of them have come to me and said, "Well, Vywamus, I really like the way things are going in your channeling classes with those wonderful human friends of yours. I, too, would like to utilize this opportunity. Will you please show me your methods and how I can work through someone in a physical body without my energy's being very difficult or exhausting for them? How can I bring the truths from the spiritual plane to humanity without confusing or unduly disrupting the channels?" I am giving classes on the spiritual plane helping the teachers utilize this wonderful opportunity so they can work with you in a gentler and easier way. I would say to you that this is why there has been so much recent attention to the channeling activity. Although it began as an experiment, I would say that from the channel's perspective, from the teacher's perspective and truly from the Earth's perspective, it really has been a great success. We are therefore taking it to a deeper and broader level and that is why we are coming forth to you now in such an open and direct way.

I hope that I have answered your questions, dear friends. I want to tell you that my mission has a lot to do with channeling. It is one of the most important things that I am doing. So if you decide that you would like to become a more active channel, a more conscious and knowing one, then I invite you to call upon me. You can just say, "Vywamus, I want to make a commitment to channeling. I really want to work with it. Come forth and help me." I can give you a visualization that might help. My energy structure is one that you might say is very encircling, very supportive. So when I am working with a channel, I like to create a bubble of energy all around him or her to encircle and support the channel's entire energy structure at all levels. I work very nicely with a sort of blue/violet energy. So if you wanted to see me in a visualization, you could imagine a great blue and violet sphere. If you like, you can give me a friendly face because I am a very friendly and loving being. If you want my assistance with your channeling just invoke me. You can bring me into your heart center and even give me a place, if you like.

I can help you with the energy of other spiritual teachers, as well. Perhaps, if you are finding that you are making a good connection energy-wise with your spiritual teacher but when the energy moves to the throat it is hard to bring it forth, I can help you strengthen the connection. If you call upon me, I will encircle you as the energy of the other teacher comes in and I will blend my energy just a little so that everything is softer and easier and comes into your structure more smoothly and powerfully. Be assured that I will never do that without the agreement of your soul and the other spiritual teachers and, most importantly, I will never connect into your space without your complete permission. We are really all working together — you, myself, your soul and the other spiritual teachers. We are working for the Light, for the glorious unfoldment of the Earth and her remarkable new children, humanity. Truly, we are also working to aid your own evolution. Remember, when you serve, you are served. That is a great universal principle.

Channeling Exercise:
Meeting the Soul and Spiritual Teacher

I, Vywamus, am pleased that you have made this commitment to channeling and I can assure you that it is most appropriate at this time. Your soul seeks to speak with you even more deeply than it has in the past. Please seat yourself comfortably, with feet or hips flat on the floor and spine straight. Go within.

Please see that you are surrounded by a beautiful column of golden Light all around your body. The Light fills you and moves through you and you feel its beauty and its support for you. Now you become aware that this beautiful column of Light descends beneath you deep down, down into the Earth. This beautiful golden Light descends down and down, farther and farther until it connects right into the heart of the Earth. You allow your conscious mind to gently descend down the column of Light, gliding, floating down the column of Light. As you descend, you see that it is bright and beautiful and there are no openings or breaks in the Light. It is strong and bright and clear. It supports you as you gently descend right to the bottom which is in the heart of the Earth.

Now with your imagination, you see that in one hand you have five beautiful golden nails of Light and in the other hand you have a golden hammer. These are the symbols of your commitment to Earth and to the Light. With the strength and power of your commitment drive the nails into the bottom of the column so that they are firm and secure and strong, connecting your column of Light deeply into the heart of the Earth. Yes, your commitment is strong and bright, my friend. You feel now a gentle, loving response from the Earth to your commitment in Light and you feel a beautiful golden-green energy flowing to you from the heart of the Earth.

This beautiful golden-green energy flows into the bottom of your column of Light and it lifts you up in the column of Light. Gliding smoothly, cradled in this beautiful loving energy from the Earth you rise up, up the column of Light right back into your body and you feel the green-golden energy moving very gently but strongly through you. Now you look up and see that your beautiful column of Light goes up and up and up through the heavens, higher and higher than you can even see. You allow your mind, your consciousness, to float up, up out of the top of your head, through the opening which is the crown chakra. Up you go, floating gently upwards in your column of beautiful golden Light and you look all around you and you see how strong, bright and clear is your golden column. There are no holes, no openings and you know within your heart that no one and nothing can come into your column of Light without your consent, for this is your place of divine connection.

Now you move upwards more quickly, gliding up and up, higher and higher, and you see that there is a bright, white Light at the top of the column, so bright and clear it touches your heart deeply and you move with joy toward it. See the bright, white, sparkling Light that calls you and moves you. You move up and up into the bright Light. You are floating high in this bright white Light of God, of the Source. You are cradled in the Light of the Source. You feel so large. You expand. Breathe deeply now, drawing in the bright white Light of the Source, filling yourself with the loving bright white Light. Now you see again that you have five golden nails in one hand and a beautiful golden hammer in the other hand and again these are the symbols of your commitment to the Source and to service of the Light. With the strength of your commitment to the Light, drive these golden nails right into the top of the column of Light so that in your imagination you can see that they are strongly anchoring this column of Light into the heart of the Source level, making a strong and powerful connection that will always be there for you.

When this is complete, begin to glide gently down, down the column of Light, floating, gliding in the Light, gently now. Looking around, see the beautiful column, strong and bright and clear, and your heart fills with the joy of this Light and its power. Now you look down and you see your physical body sitting in the column of Light. You see the crown chakra is open like a great flower and you feel yourself gently sliding through the opening at the top of your head and settling comfortably into your body again. You feel now the bright Light you have brought with you filling that body, making it feel expanded and alive, full of Light.

Now imagine that your conscious mind is a tiny human figure of Light, standing in the middle of your head. Focus all of your attention into this little being of Light until you feel that you are this figure of Light within your head.

Using your imagination, see that as you stand within the head, a beautiful stairway opens up before you going gently downward. It is a beautiful stairway of gold and white Light, sparkling brightly now, inviting, beautiful and clear. You begin to walk down the stairs and, as you walk, they become brighter and brighter. There is a soft, gentle, loving Light and it flows all around you as you move downward toward the area of your heart center.

At the bottom of the stairs you come out into a beautiful room, a beautiful, large, well-lit room with high, high ceilings full of Light. It is so beautiful! Using your imagination now, see how you have furnished and made beautiful this lovely room. There are lights and beautiful colors. Perhaps there is furniture. Perhaps there is a fountain spilling out sparkling water with a lovely tinkling sound. You see with your imagination that all the beautiful things that you have seen and loved on your journey upon the Earth are gathered here in your heart. Yes, my friends, this beautiful place of Light is your heart center. It is not just your physical heart center but it is the center of your heart energy, a great place which is the center of your being here upon Earth. From this wondrous place you can go anywhere that you desire, for this great heart is connected to All That Is. Through the heart you are connected with all the wonders that God has created and to the Source Itself.

Now, my friends, you see that in one wall is a beautiful, large door. The door is beautifully carved and there is Light streaming around its edges. You feel your heart stirring as you see the brightness and you feel a great desire to see what is beyond this beautiful door of Light. So you cross the room and you stand before the door. You look closely and see that there is a sign upon the door and you can read the sign. It says, "This is the door to the spiritual plane." Now, my friends, with the strength of your commitment to self, to your own growth as a being of Light, you open the door. Light streams all around you, beautiful white Light, and a beautiful sound of singing that is high, bright and clear fills your ears. You can hear it in the distance. Now see that you are standing in a long, beautiful corridor of Light. You see far up ahead that at the top of the corridor there is more beautiful white Light that streams in and touches your heart, stirring you with joy and hope. You begin to walk up the corridor, seeing how beautiful it is. As you walk upwards, the Light becomes brighter and brighter and the sweet high music you hear stirs your heart ever more deeply.

Now you come to the end of the hall and you step out upon a beautiful, wide plane of Light. Using your imagination, you look all around you and everywhere you see Light. There are colors dancing and flowing in the Light. Each color seems to have its own sound that sings and you feel it in your heart. You breathe deeply, drawing in the Light and the sweet, high energy of this place. You look around and you expand with joy, for you know the energy of this place. You have felt this in your heart before, but now it comes to you stronger and brighter than ever before.

You see far in the distance that there is a moving point of Light and that it is moving toward you. There is a golden path that comes right up to you and you see that a beautiful being of Light is hurrying toward you down the golden path. As it comes closer and closer, you use your imagination and you see that it is a great being of Light. There is Light flowing all around it and glorious colors trailing from it. Its energy is beautiful and strong and clear. It comes up the path and now stands before you. Using your imagination, give it a face. What kind of face would such a great being of love and Light have? Use you imagination and give it eyes that are deep and ancient and look into those eyes with your imagination and with your heart. You see an ancient wisdom that stirs your heart and you know that this one has been with you always.

You know within your heart that it is through this great being that you came forth upon the Earth. Look deeply into those loving eyes. See how strong is the love there for you. This one is committed to you and loves you. Truly, you feel trust within your heart, for this one seeks only the highest and best for you as a child of Light. You feel the trust and your heart opens to this great being. Now the being holds out its arms. If you are willing, allow yourself to be embraced. Feel yourself surrounded with the love and Light and strength of this great being. Your heart opens and its beauty, its love, and its power flow through you, filling your heart. Your heart expands and fills with joy and yes, you know who this is. You know that this one is your soul. You can feel this in your heart. Yes, you know the truth within your heart.

Feel how your heart resonates and calls to this great being. Your soul looks at you and smiles deeply. It is seeking something, asking perhaps, "Do you have a place within your heart for me?" Perhaps you do. Perhaps you have been preparing all this time, making a place, a beautiful, glorious place within your heart for this wondrous soul. If you are willing, guide your soul to the corridor that you have come through. See how it follows you in joy. See how eager this lovely being of power and Light is to connect with you, to be with you, to speak with you, to communicate and be part of your life. Glide swiftly down that corridor, your soul following you, and pass through the door back into your heart center. See? The soul does not come in. It stands at the door respecting you, respecting your free will, your choice. It waits now. It waits for you to give it permission, to invite it into your heart. No one can come into your Light without your con-

sent. Will you invite the soul into your heart now? Yes, I think
you will. Give now this invitation from your heart and ask your
soul to enter. See now how the soul in joy flows into your heart
center.

Where is the place you have made for your soul? Look around
your heart center for the perfect place you have prepared. Is it
a beautiful chair? Perhaps it is a shrine or a crystal. Indeed, my
friends, you have long been preparing this place for your soul. It
is the reason why your heart center is so beautiful. You have
been awaiting the soul. See now the place you have made for the
soul. It is so right. It is so beautiful and your love and commitment shine forth from the place you have prepared. Offer it to
your soul. See now the soul in joy and delight takes up the place
that you have prepared for it. See how perfectly you have prepared for the soul. Now sit for a while with your soul in your
heart center. If you listen within yourself, a message comes now
from your soul. You look deeply into its eyes, and using your
imagination, you see that it is conveying to you a message of love
and joy. It has waited long for this time. Listen with your heart
as your soul speaks to you now.

After you have communed with your soul until this seems complete, notice that you begin to hear a gentle sound within the
heart center. There is a knocking at the door to the spiritual
plane. There is great Light flowing around the door. Your soul
knows who is there. It is someone from the spiritual plane seeking to connect and speak with you. Your soul smiles at you, for
it knows the great and loving being that stands awaiting you in
your corridor to the spiritual plane. Will you go and see? Your
soul and you go to the door. Your soul smiles at you, reassuring
you that truly this one who comes is in the Light, is a great and
loving being. It is a spiritual teacher, perhaps a master you have
worked with before, my friend, one that you have loved and
known. Now will you open the door? I think so. Your soul en-
courages you.

See yourself opening the door. There is a great being of Light
standing there, respectfully. It is a teacher from the spiritual
plane. It does not come in because you have not yet invited it,
not yet given permission. Look closely at this wondrous being. At

first you see only a great body of Light. Now, use your imagination. What kind of face would such a great being of Light have? Give it such a face. Perhaps your secret memories will show you how that wondrous one was dressed and looked the last time you connected with it clearly. Who is this great being of Light? You look deeply into its eyes and ask. It will tell you. If you have difficulty receiving this information, listen with your heart and you will know. This spiritual teacher now seeks to connect with you again, to work with you in service to the Light. This one asks your permission to step into your heart to communicate with you. Perhaps you will allow this one to enter. I think you will, my friend, for a part of you knows this one very well. See how, as you give permission, this beautiful being of Light enters into your heart center, filling your heart with its loving, bright energy.

As you connect with it, you feel a deep trust and recognition. Truly, you know that this connection is from the Light, from the Source. If you listen very deeply, there is a message in your heart from this great teacher. If you listen, your heart will tell you what the message is. Listen to the message of love and wisdom that is being given to you. Pause now and take a little time to commune in your heart with your spiritual teacher. I believe there is also a message for you that this teacher will return to your heart center again if you will but invoke and invite.

When you feel complete with this communication, gently release the connection. The spiritual teacher embraces you lovingly and departs, but you feel that some of the beautiful Light and energy still remain with you in your heart, giving you support, hope and love. Now rest within your heart, enjoying the company, Light and love of your soul, feeling the soul's energy expanding and filling your heart. Now, my friend, begin to release the energy that you have been channeling. Begin to feel the energy releasing above your head and flowing down the top of your head, and running like water from the neck and shoulders down the back and chest, like water running away in the sand, ebbing gently, flowing away. It moves down your body down into the root chakra and moves down through the legs and feet, flowing down into the Earth. You release this bright beauteous energy that has been flowing in your column of Light into the Earth. As that Light that you have channeled touches the heart of the Earth, you feel again the loving response of the Earth and a beautiful green energy sparkling with gold comes flowing up from the heart of the Earth into your body. It flows up, filling your body gently, softly, nurturing and supporting you. This beautiful green-golden Earth energy flows right through you and out the top of your head, moving up the column of Light and into the glorious white Light of the Source at the very top of your column. You see, my friend, the Earth and the Source connect and embrace through you. Through your channel you connect them in love and Light. It is a great service that you do in this way.

Rest now in your column of Light in the heart center. Feel yourself cradled gently in the energy of your soul and the Earth. When you are ready, feel your consciousness filling up your body, your arms, your legs, your pelvis, your back, your chest, your neck, your head. You are fully occupying your body now. You are centered strongly and balanced firmly within your physical structure. Rest now and when you are ready, open your eyes.

5

Meditation for Everyone

The Beings of Light* through Ruth Ryden

There is no time like right now to consider learning how to meditate. This practice will not send you into outer space, put you into a state of complete trance or make you look like a dweeb (or any other current nerd-word).

Meditation can accomplish several things, according to your need and intention. It is a way of getting rid of modern stress and tension. It can help you get in touch with your inner being. It can be a direct line of communication with the higher-dimensional beings who are always with you, guiding, suggesting and helping you along the path of life. And it can put you into a state of total communication with the Creator of all things.

During the time you are in this state, you are still able to be completely aware of what is going on around you; you can hear, feel and see (if you have your eyes open). You have simply stepped up your conscious awareness to a point where you are more fully aware than you were before.

Why would you want to meditate? Perhaps you need to find a way to relax your mind and body because they are threatening to go out of control or because they are not responding as you know they should. It is necessary to rest the body when it is overtired and, similarly, it is also very necessary to rest the mind when it is overloaded. Just like any machine that is not taken care of regularly, the mind can find

---

*The Beings of Light are the combined thoughts of the Christ Spirit, Master Sananda, Master Hilarian, Master Kathumi, Master William and Master Peter, who incarnated as Simon Peter.

itself in a state of confusion or it can simply refuse to remember the things you need to know. Let us take you through a simple way to relax to enter the first stage of meditation.

1.   Make time — early in the morning, in the middle of the night, after the kids are in bed — any quiet time you can find. A quiet place somewhere in nature is excellent, or wherever you can be undisturbed for at least 20 to 30 minutes.

2.   The Eastern religions use a sitting position with legs crossed and hands lying quietly on the knees, palms up. The feet are tucked into a configuration that is rather difficult if you have not been trained for years to do it. Why this particular position? If you seat yourself in this manner, you will notice that you feel balanced and relaxed, and there is not much danger of falling over. The hand position is meant to bring the meditator to a balance of energy. The hands contain nerve endings that constantly bring new energy into the body. By relaxing them in a palms-up position, you are giving permission for new energy/information to flow into your mental and physical systems.

If this does not appeal to you, try sitting in a comfortable chair that supports the body and head without strain. Many people also lie on the floor, using a small pillow. Remember, however, that your subconscious mind has been trained since you were born to think that a supine position is meant for sleeping, and it is very difficult to try to meditate without falling asleep. Try different positions and see what is best for you.

One thing is important, however, and that is to keep your spine straight, whatever position you choose. Energy travels through the spine and for really effective meditation, that energy should flow in a straight line. Slouching is a bad habit, anyway.

3.   Breathing is a natural function of the body, of course, but most people have fallen into rather bad habits about it and breathe rather shallowly. If you live in a big city, that has some good points. However, in order for the body to absorb adequate oxygen into the bloodstream, deep breathing (from the diaphragm) is the way you were meant to take air into your body. Meditation requires a good supply of oxygen to the brain, so the first thing to do is breathe deeply. Fill the lungs, hold the breath for a few seconds, then exhale completely. After a few times, you will start to feel a bit light-headed,

probably; then go back to "normal" breathing. When you are exhaling from the deep breathing, let your muscles relax, a little at a time.

4. Now, this is the time to quiet the mind. Tell yourself that you are giving your mind and body a little vacation for just 30 minutes. Tell your subconscious mind to quiet down and send no mental messages for that amount of time. Tell your conscious mind to be quiet for 30 minutes. Concentrate your full attention on your feet, telling them to relax, toe by toe, if necessary. Next, do the same for the legs, thighs and hips, one leg at a time. Work through the entire body, one area at a time. Relax the shoulders and neck muscles, the head and all the little muscles around the ears and eyes at the last. You should feel like a lump of lead, with nothing capable of working at all. Perhaps a rag doll would be a good analogy. Your mind is now quiet, for you have pushed everything away except the concentration on relaxation.

5. Listen. How often how you been able to listen to complete silence? No thoughts, no strain. There is immense beauty in silence. Listen to the solar wind, the stars, the unseen energies that move all about you. Flow with the silence and float in it. If you hear far-away voices or music or see flashes of pictures, accept them and keep floating. They are nothing to fear. When the time you have set aside is coming to an end, you will begin to bring your conscious mind back to the body and take on normal feelings again. You have given this instruction to your subconscious mind and it will take care of your return to normal consciousness. Only this time, your body will feel relaxed and your mind will be more peaceful and clearer.

That's all there is to the basic principle, and if that is as far as you wish to go with it, fine. This method of mind-relaxation will help you do whatever you wish to do in your life with greater clarity and determination.

Now, if you wish to achieve higher consciousness, learn to be psychic, be able to communicate with your spiritual teachers and delve into the deepest depths of your own spiritual being, meditation is the only way to accomplish these things. Just as in anything you do in life, there must be a clear idea of what you wish to accomplish. Spiritual consciousness is no different. You cannot just dive into the ocean and immediately know how to swim. There must be the conscious determination of what you want to do, how you are going to do it and when you are going to do it. There are definite rules and regulations that are followed by all created universes. Creation is instituted in specific codes of order and if the steps are forced into unnatural patterns, there are either bad results or simply unordered confusion.

The first and most important thing you need to learn is about yourself. You are not a clump of living clay some unknown life force has turned on that returns back to nothing after its existence is completed. You are an immortal spiritual being created by the Eternal Supreme Intelligence you call God. The life force that you are is made up of the air itself, swirling about you all the time. The cells of your body are constantly being renewed and recreated. The attributes of your being were built in when you were created and are yours for all time. You can think, create and, most of all, love, for that is the reality of your being: love. You are never alone, for other spiritual beings are always beside you, helping and guiding your lifetime in matter. That inner conscience you are generally trying to ignore is the sum total of the guidance you are receiving. Listening to and following those sometimes vague feelings are the most important things you will do in your lifetimes. The more you listen, the clearer those feelings become.

They will never misguide you. No matter how loud and insistent are the media and the human voices that try to tell you how to live your lives, only your own inner guidance will tell you the unvarnished truth.

Your being is made up of three parts. The higher self (or soul self, your real base of operations); the conscious self (what you are thinking with now); and the subconscious self. The subconscious self lies deep within the conscious mind and is your managing computer, so to speak. It is programmed to run the body, play back the responses you have programmed into it, and keep in memory every word and action, every sight and sound you experience during your lifetime. It is a repository for every bad habit you have programmed into it. If you are trying to quit smoking, you are bucking your subconscious.

You can reprogram your subconscious through meditation. Remember, the first rule is to decide what you want to do. If smoking is something you wish to stop, that can be accomplished. In order to change subconscious programming, a very deep meditation must be entered into. At the point where everything is silent and deep, start concentrating on what you wish to change. It is best to use a few concise words, over and over again, as long as you can keep the concentration. Example: "I no longer have the desire to smoke." Depending upon the individual, this should have a very prompt response. You would see the desire for a cigarette lessen after just a few sessions. There are many ways to quit using chemicals and so forth, but doing it yourself will end the whole thing and give you an inner pride that cannot be purchased over the counter.

Many habits can be altered this way and each time you succeed it will be a tremendous boost to your self-esteem. Your new clarity of mind will help you to understand what you need to do next.

As you work within meditation, using concentration and learning to listen to your own guidance in many ways, you will begin to notice that what you wanted to accomplish in the first place is starting to happen by itself. When the mind is rested and clear, what you term psychic knowledge or events will begin to happen naturally. The word "psychic" is simply a term denoting the spiritual abilities and knowledge that you already have. Being psychic is simply letting those abilities happen. You cannot learn to be psychic because you already are.

As times goes on, you may very well begin to hear voices in the silence, sometimes only one or two words. It may take some thinking afterwards to figure out what they meant, but that is generally the purpose of it. Little pieces of advice or knowledge will come through from your higher self or from other spiritual advisors. Sometimes the "voice" will be like a regular sound, or it might be a knowing in the mind or a strong thought not your own. Keep listening.

Flashes, or small visions, may flit through your mind, yet remain clear and concise for a long time. These often consist of pieces of another lifetime, yours or others,' on the bands of time. They are interesting and mysterious. If your intent is to learn something of your prior lifetimes, put that intention into your mind as you drift into a deep meditation. Your higher self is always there to help you in whatever endeavor you wish to undertake. The more the concentration is held at a particular level, seeking a particular thing, the more success you will have.

Meditation is a way of life. You have probably heard of being "in constant prayer." This does not mean that a person shuffles around on his knees all the time; it is a state of recognizing that the life force is a part of the Living God and, as such, is also in constant communication with that Living God. It is a mindset that is always aware of the small nudges and helpful guidance that are constantly a part of our beings. Meditation can become so easy and so everyday that one may slip into a two- or three-minute session at odd times and still benefit tremendously from it. It is a way of making an answer clearer or of talking to your spiritual teachers about something important.

Edgar Cayce liked to say that prayer is speaking to God, and meditation is listening for the answer. Answers, however, can come in many ways. Some people never hear a word, never see a vision, but still feel the love, caring and understanding in the silence. Look back on the past year and realize how many times you have been helped in little "miraculous" ways. Things that just couldn't have happened did happen; this occurs all the time. Every time you acknowledge the help you receive, you encourage your spiritual helpers to give you more. They have no ego problems, as you do, but appreciation and love make the universe as well as the world go 'round.

We have been telling you about meditation in a very general way, giving some common examples. But realize this: meditation is an extremely personal thing. Each and every person will experience it in a different way. Your myriad experiences all through your many lifetimes have molded you into a singular being who has no equal in all of the created universes. Your training in the present lifetime has further added to the spiritual being you are. What you will experience then, deep in meditation, is given according to your own spiritual totality and can never be experienced by anyone else in exactly the same way.

The purpose you have taken on for yourself in this lifetime is being helped along by your spiritual counselors, and many times the words, thoughts or visions you receive will have something to do with helping you to achieve that purpose. If you have gone far off your path and are in some kind of danger, warnings are sometimes given in a way that you can understand. Whatever you receive from the higher dimensions is tailored for your benefit.

It must be remembered that although the experiences during meditation are extremely clear and sometimes remarkable, upon awakening they will rapidly start to fade away. This is because you have been in a higher-dimensional space and these things do not relate too well to the conscious mind. It is like the dream state. Until you have disciplined your mind to remember, it would be wise to keep a journal of some kind nearby and record what you have experienced immediately after the meditation ends. A day later, you will be glad you did, for otherwise it would have been gone.

How does all this fit in with your normal world? Not too long ago, people who meditated were treated as kooks and thought to be pretty weird. Things have changed, and are continuing to change rapidly. Huge seminars around the world are teaching people how to relax by this means and many large companies have meditation rooms set up for their employees, which is an excellent idea. Fifteen minutes of meditating rests and clears the mind far better than a cigarette break! There are few people today who deride the idea of learning to rest the mind and body. Some religions still believe this has something to do with the devil, but then, they have probably never tried it.

There is a warning to be given here. When an individual opens his or her mind to the higher dimensions, there are always those beings in spirit form who are looking for that opening. Sometimes a spirit being refuses to return to its spiritual home and is insistent upon living on Earth. It will sometimes try to enjoy that life through a still-living human being. Occasionally, this results in what is referred to as "possession," but today we see that happening far less often than in the distant past. The intelligence level of humanity has come a long way in the past hundred years and most people know instantly that something is wrong if some other force tries to take them over. Usually, this "takeover" will be on a simple level of trying to enjoy smoking or drinking, for those terrible desires and drives do not simply cease upon death of the body, but linger on in the living personality. It may take many, many Earth years before the entity can release these desires and be able to relax fully into the kingdom of love that surrounds it in its spiritual home. Let that be a brief warning.

If you receive, during meditation or at any other time you have opened yourself to a higher consciousness, information that seems scary, unreasonable or false in any way, or seems to urge you in negative directions, break off contact immediately. Direct prayer to the Creator and ask for protection and/or put the white Light around you. This will send the wayward spirit off. It would be better to wait a few days before trying again, meanwhile keeping yourself surrounded by love. Remember, there is nothing in heaven or on Earth that can withstand the power of God! Fear is in the mind of man, not in the mind of God.

There are many meditation tapes on the market today, and they can be of great help. It is difficult to concentrate on the mechanics of working with the mind when the day's problems are whirling in an unending spiral. The tapes help by giving you something else to listen to and directions to follow. The relaxation sessions are a good way to learn how to release the tensions of the day, and the visualizations are fun and sometimes very inspiring. There can be too much of a good thing here, however. You can spend the next ten years working with these tapes and never get closer to your inner self. When the silence is achieved and the mind and body are relaxed, turn off the tape and proceed as directed above. These tapes make a lot of money for their authors and most of them are made with the best of intentions, but they cannot do for you what you can do for yourself. We see far too many groups using interesting tapes during group sessions when they should be combining their meditative energies on a specific thought or project.

Meditation, properly used, results in a strong force of energy. It has to in order to achieve what it does. When two or more persons combine their time and energies at the same instant, that force becomes even more powerful. Peace initiatives, awareness of the need for the preservation of the Earth, the stopping of possible atomic wars, all have happened because of the combined strength of millions of people meditating and praying together. There is nothing so beautiful as the peaceful and powerful feelings generated by a meditating group of aware people. This is what truly pulls people together in love and trust. There can be no spite or hate or deception in such a group; it is a healing and growing force of love. This is why small groups accomplish so much more: One does not attend such a group unless he or she has the intention of growing in knowledge and awareness. Large church groups contain many people who attend for social or political reasons and the cohesive energies that cement small groups simply do not exist. If you cannot find a group where you live, try to find one other person who is willing to study, pray and meditate with you. In a short time, others will find you!

We'd like you to consider this: there are times in the lives of all of you when everything goes wrong, when seemingly unreasonable and unaccountable accidents happen that completely turn around your lives and the lives of those you love, shaking the very foundations of life as you know it. You are told over and over that everything happens because you created it, one way or another. For the most part, this is true.

But there are accidents. There are terrible things happening in your world that have nothing to do with you or your own determination of where your life is going. The variations in the endless multitudes of tiny events occurring every moment of time are too complicated even for those of us in the higher dimensions of time. A lifetime that has been well planned out before incarnation can be completely upset and destroyed because of a simple mistake or an accident caused by someone else. Yes, this happens. That lifetime then becomes an even greater challenge to that entity whose higher self gives as much help as possible to make a learning experience out of it. This is not all that tragic, however, since each soul entity lives through countless lifetimes in many dimensions, during many times and on many planets. It is normal that a few of these lifetimes fail in one way or another. If this has happened to you or someone you love, it is time to realize that new plans need to be made for that lifetime; it is time to release old desires, needs or plans, and time to look ahead for the viable possibilities that lie there. If a lifetime in a wheelchair, for instance, is substituted for a sports career, it takes some extremely strong intentions to quiet the rage and grief and achieve the difficult determination to learn acceptance. Then, and only then, will the inner being be able to start sending new guidance and help.

Meditation is the best way in the world to regain the balance such tragedies destroy in the human spirit. It is not an escape from the cruel, cruel world, but an entrance to new strength and wisdom. Living a very physical, busy and productive lifetime is wonderful, but the benefits of living a very mental lifetime have given the world new technologies, beautiful music and wisdom beyond compare. Life is much more than a beautiful face and a strong set of muscles. When you have visited your higher being in meditation, this is easy to realize. One of the most accomplished mathematicians in the world cannot move his body at all, but his mind has given the world what a physically able man could not.

Meditation can be used as a point of concentration for the mind and subconscious mind to heal the body. It is no secret today that the mind controls the body. Emotions, hatred and resentments are making a mess out of humanity, but humanity is beginning to realize it. There are many fine people, doctors, therapists and so on, who are working with people to help them use their own minds to heal their ills. Meditation is the key factor here, for the intense concentration used in these methods is the only way to reach the deepest parts of the mind that control the bodily functions. Using this method yourselves, before you become ill, is simply constantly affirming that your body is in perfect condition, functioning as it should and that there is nothing that can harm it. You don't think that would work? Just try it over a few months. You will never feel so well.

Look at meditation from many angles, and you will see how much the human race is beginning to learn and depend upon it for the truth and knowledge that are sought for so earnestly now. Every man and woman needs it in different ways and will benefit from it in different ways. Search your heart, your desires and even your physical needs to see if this is not something that will help you.

There is never a time when your need for an inner commitment to yourself is not important in your life. Living your life as though you were forever sailing in a boat on the ocean of life and never knowing or understanding the myriad life forms beneath you is foolish and boring. Too many people have lived and will live their lives this way, searching, always searching, for something exciting and worthwhile, while all the time it is really there, inside them, and they never know it. We sincerely hope you will take on the adventure of the totality of life within yourselves, in others and in the recognition of the ongoing creation of life itself.

God bless you all.

Recommended Reading

Cooke, Grace. *Meditation.* Marina del Rey, CA: DeVorss, 1955.

Maharishi Mahesh Yogi. *Transcendental Meditation.* New York: NAL-Dutton, 1988.

Puryear, Herbert B. & Thurston, Mark A. *Meditation and the Mind of Man.* Virginia Beach, VA: A.R.E. Press, 1975.

Stearn, Jess. *The Power of Alpha Thinking.* New York: NAL-Dutton, 1977.

6

Spirit Guides

Ai Gvhdi Waya

I was taught by Sam, my Cherokee teacher, that each person, whether Indian or not, has a chief guide or spirit guide. I had always likened my spirit guide to the Christian idea of a guardian angel who is always there to help us, counsel us, and in general keep us out of hot water, provided we listen to the voice of our spirit guide or our intuition, our knowing, if you will. The spirit guide is called a deva by those who follow other metaphysical disciplines.

True, the angelic kingdom is a separate kingdom from what I'm going to share with you, but this is the closest I can come from my own shamanic/Cherokee training to giving those outside of my view of the world an idea of what I am talking about.

So, let's start at the beginning. I was taught that each person has a spirit guide, a chief one, who oversees our development during this lifetime. This spirit guide, at least for those of Native American heritage (and I will stick my neck out and suggest that it is also true for those people who have had strong incarnations as North or South American Indians), always comes in the guise of an animal, insect, reptile or plant.

I remember one conversation with Sam about chief spirit guides. One of my friends had told me that his was a bald eagle. I was taught to look at what the animal, in this case a bird, would mean. My teacher told me to look at the guide in the context of what it was, what it did and how it moved within the flow of the river of life that surrounds all of us, whether we're two-leggeds, four-leggeds, winged ones, crawlies, plants or little people (the insect kingdom). When my teacher told me this, I know I gave him a very perplexed look. He asked me what the bald eagle did and I replied, "It flies."

"What else?" he prompted.

I searched frantically for a better answer, for flying was obvious.

"Well...uh, it flies higher than any other bird in the world."

"That's true. What else?"

I began to sweat. What else does an eagle do?

"Uh," I stammered, "it eats fish because it's a sea eagle."

"Yes. What else?"

Frantic, I seesawed between anger toward my teacher for being so pedantic and desperation because I was trying to please him by coming up with the right answer. I didn't like this kind of prodding, but he just patiently stood there, looking at me while I sweated.

"Let's see...." I rolled my eyes upward to Father Sky, searching for the answer. I wrestled for nearly five minutes, the silence growing heavy between us. He finally took pity on me.

"How does it hunt?"

Wiping the sweat off my face, I scrunched up my brow. "The eagle flies high to see the fish in the water and then swoops down to grab it out of the water with its claws."

"Good," he praised.

"Thank goodness," I thought.

"But, what else?"

I grimaced and gave him a pleading look. "I don't know what else."

He smiled. "Sometimes surrendering is better than scrambling for an answer."

Grinning sheepishly, I acknowledged his wisdom. If I'd been honest with myself, I'd have said from the beginning that I didn't know. That's at least surrendering over to the truth, which is something he was trying to teach me to do. I remembered another old adage: "Pride goeth before a fall." Well, I had had a fall.

Sam gestured to the sky. "What is the bald eagle's strongest point? What does he do best besides fly?"

I thought and thought. Finally, in a moment of desperate inspiration I said, "His eyes! He's got excellent vision."

Sam's smile broadened significantly. "Yes!"

Catching his enthusiasm, I began waving my hands around because that's what I do when I'm excited or trying to explain something either to myself or another person. "An eagle's eyes are his most important attribute. So are you saying a person whose chief spirit guide is an eagle has good eyes."

"Now, the whole reason you get a spirit guide is to become like it," Sam counseled.

"Oh, that means the person may not see things well, then?"

"Yes, but the eagle will teach her or him how to see things better and with more depth or perception and, perhaps, clarity."

Excited, I nodded, beginning to grasp the relationship he wanted me to understand.

"So the bald eagle would be a symbol, telling this person to aspire to become like the bird?"

"Yes." He gave me a look of praise. "Remember, when we become aware of our chief spirit guide, the real training, the changes and transformation, begin to take place."

"But," I struggled, "what if the person doesn't want to see? Or what if he doesn't want to learn to 'fly' above a situation to see it more clearly?"

Sam thought. "The chief spirit guide is with us from the moment we're born until we leave our physical form and even after that, in some cases. This bald eagle wouldn't force his or her human counterpart to change if he or she didn't want to. A chief spirit guide is there to be listened to through our inner voice, our heart, our feelings and intuition. If we choose not to listen, then that's our problem."

"And then," I guessed, "those people will run into a lot of road blocks and walls in their lives?"

"Yes."

"Sam, what else could this bald eagle possibly symbolize?"

He grinned and squinted up at me from where he crouched on the ground. Scooping up some dirt, he allowed it to sift through his large, weathered hands. "What do you feel about it?"

I groaned and plopped down in front of him, my legs crossed. "I knew you were going to answer a question with a question!"

Laughing, he continued to sift the dirt, handling it as if it were a very much loved child. "So? What do you feel?"

Grumpily, I stared down at Mother Earth, my chin resting in the palms of my hands. "It flies. So, what does flying mean symbolically?" I was thinking out loud so he could see my thought process.

"Flying could mean rising above a situation to see it more clearly. Or it could mean letting go of my own reality, teachings given to me by school, parents or religion. If I could do that, maybe I could perceive my situation, whatever it was, in a new or different light, a better one?" I twisted a look up at his darkly tanned face. I saw the wrinkles at the corners of his eyes grow pronounced, so I knew he was pleased with my answer — thus far. Sighing, I went on. "There's the saying that if you stick with the turkeys, you'll never fly like an eagle."

Sam laughed out loud, the deep, resonating sound echoing around the canyon where we sat. "So what does that mean?"

"That if I have this chief spirit guide, I'm supposed to reevaluate my parental conditioning process and the environment I've been raised in and look at my philosophy to see what can be thrown out and what can be kept."

"Why?"

"I knew you were going to ask that," I said unhappily, giving him a dirty look. He was smiling, so I knew I was on the right track. After ruminating for several minutes, I said, "The whole Native American experience is about learning to be always in harmony and in balance within ourselves," I said. "And to do this, we must remember that not everything we were taught or were trapped within helps us to achieve that goal. In order to do it, we must let go of these things that hinder us, keep us unbalanced or stop us from growing."

"Right so far. Go on," he drawled.

Quirking my lips, I muttered, "That's so easy for you to say."

"Wait until you have students of your own," he said, smiling.

I wasn't thinking of my students. In fact, I'd never thought along those lines. I gave him a startled look, but I saw his eyes grow distant and I knew he wasn't going to say any more than he already had. "Okay," I groused belligerently, "the key word here is 'transformation,' with the goal being our own unique balance and harmony within ourselves. So, if I got a bald eagle for a chief spirit guide, I'd probably have to look very closely at my upbringing and beliefs and begin to honestly throw out what was no longer useful to me or stopped me from growing spiritually. The eagle would help me to rise above my own limitations, to see more clearly in order to make better choices that would help me grow in a positive way.

"Very good. What about the bald eagle flying higher than any other bird?"

"You've always said that eagles flew higher than anyone else and that they had the ear of the Great Spirit because of that. They're also messengers."

"That's right. How would you interpret that?"

Groaning, I said, "If I transformed, grew and listened to my own inner guidance, to my heart through which the chief spirit guide speaks, I might communicate more closely with the Great Spirit?"

"Yes." Sam slowly unwound his lean, tall form and stood up. He had a piece of grass stuck in the corner of his mouth. He was chewing on it thoughtfully. "Not only that, but if you work hard, listen and walk through your fear of transformation, you may someday become a messenger from the Great Spirit to others." He looked down at me and his eyes twinkled. "That is a very honored and humbling position to be in."

"Very," I murmured. I stood up and brushed the seat of my pants off, knowing the day's lesson was finished. Sam was a very powerful Cherokee medicine man, but he was humble about it, too, and I was always conscious that those who had real power were the humblest of us all. At least those who were walking in harmony had left their egos behind and moved with the flow of the river of life.

Discovering My Spirit Guide

I didn't have to worry about having an eagle as a chief spirit guide. I had discovered mine nearly twenty years earlier when I had come upon a blue-gray wing-tip feather. You see, we all have a chief spirit guide, a deva, if you will, who is our mentor throughout our lifetime. Sometimes we'll see this chief spirit guide in physical form. For instance, you might see a squirrel three times in a very short space of time, perhaps days, or see a red-tail hawk three days in a row, or a coyote.

That is how the devic kingdom "talks" to us — either though physical manifestation, showing up in our lives three times in a row, or by coming to us in a dream, vision or meditation. Native Americans always put great stock in the number three, and if we see anything three times in a row, we're paying attention because we know this animal is trying, first, to get our attention, second, to "talk" to us, and third, to get us to take the symbolic form and apply it to our lives. Let me give you an example.

I was walking one night with my husband, arm in arm, on the fifteen-acre Arabian horse farm we had in Lisbon, Ohio. Naturally, our nine horses were following us, single file, as we took our evening stroll. It was a time to talk with my husband, trade what had happened during the day and, in general, have "quality time" with one another. On this particular evening it was near dusk as we walked the large oval fields. I spotted a long gray-blue feather. Enchanted, I rushed forward to look at it. How beautiful and huge it was! My husband came up and looked down at it. My heart began pounding. I didn't know why at the time.

I felt trembly all over, and a good kind of excitement came over me as I leaned down to look at it more closely. I was struck by its lovely pale blue color. I had no idea what kind of feather it was, but I did know that it was significant. As I reached down, I told my husband that if I picked up the feather, my life would begin to change drastically. I didn't know why I'd said that or why I knew that; I simply knew it to be true. And without hesitation, I gently picked up the "finger feather." The moment I did, a great blue heron flashed in front of the view screen located in the center of my head. I told my husband this feather belonged to a great blue heron.

He reminded me that a great blue heron always fished in the small creek that flowed through our property. I stood there, my fingertips tingling as I lightly stroked that incredibly long, lovely feather. It was then that I remembered: I would often be out on the swing under the cottonwood tree in the evenings, just absorbing the ending of the day, when a great blue heron would fly in with her magnificent seven-foot wingspan and land in the creek just below our farmhouse. She had been doing that for seven years in a row, but I hadn't realized why she kept visiting me. I guess I was too dense and didn't get the message of her visits, so she had to drop a wing-tip feather in the pasture to get my attention.

It has been many years since I picked up that feather. I had been right. My life did change dramatically. Within a year, my teacher, Sam, came into my life. The great blue heron, I found out later, was my chief spirit guide, and since then I've been learning how to become a great blue heron in my life. The devic kingdom embraces all of the Great Spirit's animals, insects, reptiles, plants, rocks, water, and even Mother Earth herself. Why should we not be able to learn and grow through that which nurtures us the most? Mother Earth is our true mother. She feeds us, clothes us and cares for us. When Native Americans say, "all our relatives" or "all my relations," we mean simply that we are all interconnected with one another, without exception.

The River of Life Unites Us

The river of life, invisible (to our naked eyes) rainbow-colored energy, flows in, around and through us, permeating every cell of our bodies. It touches all forms of life and this includes Mother Earth herself. That is how we are bound to one another, and what we do to ourselves sends out a vibrational frequency that affects many others on many other levels, both seen and unseen.

We all have a chief spirit guide. If you'd like to know how to get in touch with yours, think back and ask yourself, "What has happened to me three times in a row in a very short time?" If you can't think of anything, then tell your subconscious just before you go to sleep at night, "I want my chief spirit guide to contact me through a dream." Do this for at least thirty days. It might not happen at first, but eventually, your perseverance will be rewarded. Or if you meditate, ask the same thing and see what happens. Another, perhaps easier, way is to have a shaman journey for you and find out on your behalf, keeping in mind that he or she must have permission to do it — yours and that of a higher authority! If you are indeed sincere about wanting to know who your chief spirit guide is, your question will be answered eventually. Part of the Red Road experience is learning patience and endurance.

There is a hierarchy I was taught. Besides the deva, or chief spirit guide, there is a lesser pantheon of spirit guides for us, also in animal form, that come and go in our lives. These transitory devas/animal spirit guides are less powerful than the chief deva/spirit guide, but they come into our lives to teach us an individual skill that we're ready to learn. Now, we may not consciously be aware that we're ready to learn this new thing. I try to pay attention to what it is. I then ask myself, "What does this guide symbolize? How can I apply it to my own experience right now?"

Let me give you an example. Let's say a flicker comes into my life, and that I see this bird three times in a row on the same day. First, I would go to the library and read up on this bird to find out what her characteristics are. Once I found out, I'd ask myself how they apply to me. For instance, a flicker survives by having a long, narrow beak that bores holes into the bark of trees to find little bugs hiding in there. From a symbolic standpoint, it would mean focus, wouldn't it? Drilling in one spot to create a hole to go after a particular thing or goal is certainly focus, intensity and single-minded purpose, isn't it? The promise of the flicker is this: if I concentrate on one thing long enough, with patience and endurance, I will get the "gift" of the bug. I would look at what I'm currently doing in my life and ask, "What do I need to concentrate on single-mindedly until I complete the task and get the gift?" Such is the lesson of the flicker if she enters your life. There are many other symbolisms regarding the flicker, but this one will suffice as an example. When you have learned the new skill or lesson, the lesser spirit guide leaves you. Then, at some point in the future, the deva will bring another one into your life to symbolize the next rung on the ladder of your growth.

A good resource for understanding some of the symbolism is medicine cards, as well as your own footwork at the local library and asking naturalists, zoo-keepers or people who know the specific animal's traits.

Change Is Our Responsibility

The chief spirit guide is there to help us, guide us and speak to us in the language of the right brain — the heart, feelings and intuition or inner voice. If we elect to transform and grow, then other spirit guides will be asked to come to us to teach us certain new skills, embellish a talent, nurture us or support us in some new endeavor. However, if we allow fear to stop us, the chief spirit guides cannot force us to change — that's not their responsibility. It's ours. What *is* a chief spirit guide's responsibility is to be there to support us and act as an inner counsel for us. Plus, they bring in other "teachers," new spirit guides, as we grow to a place where we can expand, add to our skills or develop new ones.

All of these phenomena are deva-based — the spirit guides, the river of life, our Mother Earth. Having the courage to break the hold of the fear(s) that stop us from being all that we can be is up to us. I can tell you unequivocally that there is a cheering section for each of you, unseen, who are rooting nonstop for you to "leap tall buildings in a single bound." If you have the courage to make the change, the inner support will be there.

The Rose Devas

Besides a personal group of spirit guides for each of us, there are also devas all over Mother Earth who function in harmony with her and all our relations. Let me give you an example. I have a large rose garden, most of the plants being tree roses or huge rose bushes. There is a deva who is "in charge" of the entire group of rose bushes, some forty of them. Each rose bush has its own spirit. These individual spirits work willingly with the deva who oversees them. The deva is nurturing, supportive and helpful. The "elementals," less evolved forms of spiritual energy who most often appear to be balls of Light, flow in the river of life. The rose garden deva makes sure that elemental energy is there to "feed" each individual rose bush and also to ensure the continual flow of the river of life's energy through and around each rose bush. My job is to water the roses, prune them and give them fish fertilizer.

I'm in mental contact with the rose garden deva. As I go around to each rose bush, I touch the plant, talk to it, praise it and tell it how beautiful it is. I can feel each rose plant respond with such incredible love that it brings tears to my eyes. Every day I go out there and touch them, love them and praise them. So, I'm doing more than just watering them and giving them fertilizer. The rose bushes flower from February through November each year! Granted, I live in Arizona, but we're at 3,500 feet, and we get snow sometimes, so believe me, roses blooming in November is a minor miracle in itself!

Every time you see a mountain, remember there is a mountain deva who is charged with caring for all the rock people, each of whom has a spirit, so you know there are millions of devas, one for each of the rocks that make up a mountain! Each vicinity on Mother Earth has a deva who is in charge, who ensures the harmony, the flow of the river of life through that area. A river has a deva, just as a stream has a spirit. The larger the river, the more powerful the deva. The larger the mountain, the more powerful the deva, and so on. We have a fifty-tree fruit orchard, and there is a fruit tree deva who is there to help nurture each of those trees.

You all have devas where you live. Each tree has a living spirit in it, each rock, each flower, each bush. If you'd like to contact a deva, I'll share with you what I was taught.

1. Start in your own back yard. Go outside when you feel at peace with yourself — don't do this if you're angry, upset or distracted. What this demands of you is flicker medicine: single-minded purpose and concentration. Take a braid of sweetgrass and light it. Wave it around the area. Sweetgrass is a "perfume" to devas and elementals; they love the aroma of it. Elementals will eagerly come because they see you are honoring them and respecting them and gifting them.

2. Burn at least half a rope of sweetgrass and then close your eyes. Take three deep breaths into the nostrils and out of the mouth. Center yourself. Give your name (a very important thing to do) and tell the spirits that you have come to gift them and honor them. Then, wait. The Cherokee have a great saying: "Expect nothing, receive everything." Just wait. After about twenty minutes, open your eyes, burn the rest of the sweetgrass rope and say, "Thank you for coming. I honor you." Have a notebook with you so you can journal your experience: any sensations, emotions, physical or mental responses, any colors, symbols or words spoken. Write them down.

Patience Is the Key

3. You may have to do this at least three times before anything will happen. I'm not going to tell you what can happen, because I don't want to set you up, psychologically. Many devas and elementals have been hurt and injured by man, so at this point they are naturally distrustful of most human beings on first encounter. However, if you show them your intent by gifting them with sweetgrass, then that's a signal that you're "safe" and that you're coming from the heart. Gradually, they will come closer and closer. The elementals are highly curious and will probably be the first to "touch" you. The devas are more circumspect because they are much more evolved and more watchful and they know what lies in your heart and whether you really are sincere about contacting them. A deva will know your true intent. So, if you're doing this out of curiosity or for selfish purposes, they'll never come up and introduce themselves to you. However, if you are sincere, a deva will test you — for how long, it's hard to say. They want to make sure you want to contact them. Patience is the key here.

4.   Another way to draw elementals and devas to you is to sing them songs or play a musical instrument for them. They love singing! You can light the sweetgrass and hum or sing. I use a drum, and I also have a flute I play (poorly, believe me, but it's the intent that counts!).

5.   Once you have made contact with the deva, ask what you can do for her/him/it. Would it like you to come once a week and sing a song? Play a drum or some other musical instrument you're skilled at? Dance with it? Meditate and visualize a certain color in harmony with it? The possibilities are endless. In return, a deva can become your teacher; but this isn't something you ask, expect or demand from them. In order to get, you've got to give. You have to prove to the deva that you're coming sincerely from your heart and want nothing except to give the outpouring of love, respect and honor that come from the deepest part of you.

6.   I was also taught to leave gifts of food behind — and not meat, either! Grain, seeds and berries can be offered so that the deva can call to the bird people to come and eat, can ask the squirrels, chipmunks or mice to share in the gift, too. By giving, you will automatically, over time, receive something of equal (and usually greater) value. Be open and receptive.

7.   If a deva takes you "under its wing" many wonderful and positive things can happen. It is like teamwork; you help one another. There is a sense of sharing and joy like none other you have experienced. Further, a deva can "talk" to you in your dreams, in meditation, in a vision or, if you're clairvoyant, you'll feel them impressing you with mental telepathy and feelings.

The Sequoia Deva

I have one last experience, about a sequoia deva, that I'd like to leave you with. Many years ago, Sam sent me to the sequoia groves up above Bakersfield, California. I had an incredible experience with one particular sequoia spirit. He gave me his name and asked if he could work with me. I said yes. A week after I returned home to Lisbon, Ohio, one of my favorite horses, Molly, got colic which is a stomach ache only a lot more dangerous.

Molly rolled and flailed around in the paddock next to the barn, grunting and groaning. I was beside myself with terror because I knew she didn't have just plain old colic, but a deadly form known as "twisted gut colic" that usually ends up killing a horse. The only way a horse could be saved was an expensive (thousands of dollars) operation. But we lived so far out in the country, and I knew our veterinarian didn't have the facilities to perform such an operation. I ran to the house to call Dick, our vet. The assistant said he was out on another emergency call. I'm afraid I wasn't cool, calm or collected. I sobbed into the phone that Dick had to come right now! I slammed down the phone and tore back out to the paddock where Molly was continuing to roll in horrible agony.

I tried to stop Molly from rolling because in twisted gut colic, it only makes the situation worse. However, trying to stop a one-thousand pound horse from rolling when I was only one hundred and forty pounds, not to mention the flailing, deadly hooves, is no easy task. I didn't succeed. Frantically, I tugged and pulled on her halter, trying to get her to stand and walk which would have helped. But Molly was in such pain that all she could do was roll, groan and grunt. Twenty minutes passed. Molly had broken out in a heavy sweat, her skin glistening. I raced back to the house and called the vet again. He was still out! This time, I shrieked at the receptionist to get him here or Molly was going to die!

I ran back to the paddock, knowing that Molly was going to die. I was crying so much by the time I reached her that I stumbled and fell into the dirt beside her. Molly stopped only momentarily, heaving for breath, groaning, her eyes rolling back in her head. The moment I tried to get her up, she started rolling again. Forty-five minutes passed. By this time, Molly was getting tired, foam covering her chest and flanks, but she still rolled ceaselessly. I called the vet a third time. He was on his way! I ran back out to the paddock, terrified, knowing it was too late.

Molly lay on her side, panting and groaning, so weak now that she was resting between bouts of rolling. Sobbing so hard I couldn't see, I fell down by her side and placed both my hands on her belly. I was desperate. I would try anything. I called to the sequoia deva and asked for his help. The instant I asked, I saw an incredible green Light snaking up and out of Mother Earth right under us and moving up through my body and out of my hands. I watched in amazement as the green Light flooded in web-like strands all across Molly's belly. My sobbing stopped. My tears dried. I knelt there feeling incredible energy pumping up through me, vibrating me; I saw it completely encircle Molly's belly. I vaguely heard Molly give an "ommphhhh." The mare suddenly groaned, released a long sigh through her nostrils, and then, miraculously, she relaxed. Her entire body went slack. Horrified, my eyes flew open and I looked at her, thinking she'd died. Her eyes were half open, and she was still alive.

The green Light began to thin out to a trickle, and in another five minutes, it had disappeared. I heard my sequoia deva tell me that Molly would be fine. Sniffing, I lifted my trembling hands from her belly and watched her. She was utterly relaxed, breathing normally and no longer in pain. I could scarcely believe it.

Then I realized that in my state of high anxiety, I'd forgotten to ask for help. I'd been so upset, I'd forgotten to ask anybody but the vet. I knelt there by Molly in a state of shock. I hadn't known tree devas could do something like this! Gathering my wits, I stumbled to my feet and rushed back to the farmhouse to tell the vet that he didn't have to come.

As I hurried back to the paddock after making the five-minute call, my heart stopped. Molly was gone! She was not in the paddock! How could that be? Panicked, I ran into the barn. There, in the stall, Molly was contentedly munching on hay! My mouth fell open. I just couldn't believe it. Anyone who owns horses or has had a colicky one knows that they never eat right after a colic; it takes hours for them to get over their stomach ache.

I rushed into the stall, hands shaking as I touched Molly in disbelief. She was no longer sweating. She wasn't nervous or exhausted at all! I stood there, absolutely stunned. I knew then that the sequoia deva had healed Molly completely and to the point where she appeared never to have had the colic in the first place!

I heard the screech of tires entering the barn driveway. It was the vet! What was I going to tell him? I heard him slam the car's door. He was running toward the barn entrance. I ran to meet him. Dick halted, bag in hand, wide-eyed and breathing hard. I threw up my hands and told him it was all right. And then I stammered through an explanation, leaving out the healing portion, of course.

"It's impossible for Molly to recover that quickly," he told me as we hurried to her stall. Taking out his stethoscope, Dick listened intently to her stomach for gut sounds, an indication that the colic was gone. I stood there tensely, watching him closely as he checked her belly, checked her heart rate, looked at her eyes and walked around her with a scowl on his brow.

"Well," Dick muttered, "this just can't be."

"What can't?"

"She's fine. It's as though you were making up the story. There's no sign of colic. Her gut sounds are normal. Her heart rate is normal and so is her breathing." He gave me a searching look. Dick and I had been working together for almost five years, and he knew I was competent in vetting my horses and would never lie to him about something like this.

I felt my face getting very red and hot and I shrugged my shoulders. "I guess it's a miracle, Dick." And it was. A sequoia deva miracle.

Recommended Reading

Ingerman, Sandra. *Soul Retrieval.* San Francisco: Harper Collins, 1991.

Harner, Michael. *The Way of the Shaman.* New York: Bantam Books, 1982.

7

Walk with the Angels: Aliens and ETs

Reverend Helga Morrow

Discussing aliens and ETs with an audience familiar with such phenomena is relatively easy. My audiences usually nod affirmatively and can identify with some of my experiences because they are similar to their own. However, such people have had to overcome criticism of their beliefs and the conditioning of centuries by churches, parents and peers. I have not found that to be a problem, as I've been receptive to the unexplained since I was a toddler and by now I'm quite matter-of-fact about strange happenings.

In order for the uninitiated to understand what I am about to say you may have to simply think as a child and grow into these experiences, as I have. That way you don't over-analyze or use unnecessary jargon that will confuse your thoughts.

I will let you follow me through my life starting with my childhood and moving forward to this very moment. To begin with, I was fortunate because I had parents who refrained from criticizing me, mocking me or putting fear into my unusual experiences.

My first alien/ET visit occurred at the age of two when I had "outside help" with early reading and writing from what I thought at the time was an angelic being. This being had dark skin and wavy black hair. He wore tight black satin pants with a flowing, cream-colored "poet shirt" that had bouffant sleeves. He would come to me and actually whisper into my ear the words I was reading. To the amazement of my parents, this Peter Pan creature took me soaring all over the world, to castles and cathedrals and even to my grandmother's home in Germany. "Remote viewing" is what this is called today.

I learned a lot from my alien friend. One of the things I did was to sit in bed and channel beings in another country who were speaking another language. I was able to speak fluent ancient Finnish, describing my surroundings in that country during another lifetime. Did the alien or angel trigger these episodes or did they come naturally? But then, what is natural?

I soon learned to trust what I saw and heard. This is the key, I think. Not only did my parents observe me doing this, but they listened to me without criticism. I soon learned that friends of my own age didn't understand. So, rather than be ostracized by my peers, I stopped sharing my stories with them.

That was over fifty years ago. What about today? Despite the rampant sex and violence in the media, alien encounters are still whispered about. Although I refuse to be a crusader or to stand on a soap-box, I would love to see more open-mindedness on such subjects now, after all this time has passed. Despite the unwillingness and fear of some, I am telling you the unvarnished truth as I have been shown it.

Yes, I have been visited. I have come to the conclusion that there is a good reason for our being contacted. Many people have been taught to shut out the memory of having been contacted, but more and more people are becoming curious, and those people need to know it's okay to learn about these subjects and to speak about them now.

Some of us like to go back to our childhoods, recalling memories of beautiful dreams. Or were they visitations? Think like a child. Find that little girl or boy who will walk with "angels."

Now you are ready; now you can recognize "them."

When I was six years old, I first met what I then thought was my guardian angel. In reality, he was my alien guide, and he has been with me for over fifty years. I trust him completely. He has fair skin, blue eyes and white-blond flowing hair and he wears a glittery white jumpsuit. He is over six feet tall and has a strong masculine voice. His messages and unfailing guidance have shown me there is more to our existence than the information fed to us by the schools, the pulpits and the media.

My first "contact" showed me his ship. He has told me of changes that are to come and he is fulfilling the promise he made to me and others aboard a huge craft hovering over Sedona's Thunder Mountain in April of 1991. I will share it with you:

"Go forth and do research, but make sure that it will not only excite your higher consciousness but also realign your purpose. You must not only change your previous Earthly goals and begin to work for the betterment of mankind. You must also change your way of thinking if you are to be given a second chance. It all boils down to attitude. It doesn't matter if you are crippled in body; as long as you have the right attitude, you will be given a chance to be whole again. It doesn't matter who you are or what you become in life, but how you have achieved your goals. Success and prosperity are achieved first in the mind, but it is more important to give love, time and devotion to service to your fellow man.

"Be loyal to your primary belief structure: Christ, Buddha and countless others have followed this path. You can emulate them to achieve your heavenly rewards.

"Do not break your commitment to the Supreme Power whom you know as God. If you are worthy in God's eyes, you will be one of the chosen ones given eternal life, immortality.

"Go forth to be leaders of men. You here in this room were chosen because of your attitude. Constant contemplation is a key factor in correctly attuning your attitude. The followers will hold stubbornly to their negative attitudes; only the teachable ones and the leaders will be rewarded with life everlasting. God, the Supreme Power, is using you to perpetuate the Divine Plan. We have armies of angelic beings. We tune into each and every one of you. We are real; we have been divinely present throughout history.

"Remember that you are divine. You can change the future through prayers and positive thoughts. Focus only on pure mind and spiritual thoughts. These thoughts, these Godly attitudes, will move mountains.

"We have always been. We shall always remain."

Recommended Reading

Dongo, Tom. *The Alien Tide*. Sedona, AZ: T. Dongo, 1990.

Elders, Brit, Elders, Lee and Welch, Thomas. *UFO...Contact from the Pleiades*, Vol. I. Munds Park, AZ: Genesis III Publishing, 1980.

Meier, Billy. All books by and about this man are excellent.

Nichols, Preston and Moon, Peter. *The Montauk Project: Experiments in Time*. Westbury, NY: Sky Books, 1992.

Sitchin, Zecharia. *The Twelfth Planet* (and subsequent books of *The Earth Chronicles*). Santa Fe: Bear & Co., 1991.

8

UFOs: A Case in Point

Virgil Armstrong

U FOs. We all have to start some place in our awareness of
them, just as I did. It is hoped that an understanding of
my path of realization will be helpful to you.

Forty-five years ago when I was a young Army captain I was
involved in the second capture of an extraterrestrial spacecraft here in
the USA. I never in my wildest dreams sensed that as a result of this
experience — and many more to follow — I would become internation-
ally sought after for my understanding and knowledge of UFOs and
extraterrestrial activities.

Perhaps my acceptance of things extraterrestrial as normal was
spawned during my rich association with and learning from the Native
American peoples during more than 23 years. The Native American
sees nothing unusual in the existence and periodic appearance of
extraterrestrial craft and peoples and very nonchalantly refers to them
as "our brothers, the Sky People."

Indian verbal memorabilia is rich in allusion to things extraterrestrial, rendering the state of affairs here on Earth commonplace. In
an oblique way, they imply that extraterrestrial association and understanding are indeed more real and permanent than terrestrial affairs.

We, the purportedly civilized and learned ones, are so steeped in
our own narrow intelligence and fixed beliefs and ways that, indeed,
we are the ignorant and misguided ones who virtually drown in our
preconceived misconceptions and linear thinking and actions. Often,
people and some religious groups in particular vehemently declare
that the subject of UFOs is nonsense and the work of the devil, to be

avoided at all costs. Despite what these groups feel they must say or do, it is difficult to follow their line of reasoning once one has become a direct player in the whole range of ufology.

Upon my first awareness that there was such a thing as a UFO, I was not duly impressed and said to my contemporaries, "Why not? Surely there must be other intelligences, some greater than ours, in God's creation and universe! We can't be the only ballgame in this wide expanse of the heavens!"

As I've implied, my first awareness that there were UFOs occurred in 1948. I was a young Army captain, age 24, assigned to high-level intelligence because of my wartime expertise. At the time of the incident I am about to relate, I was on loan for temporary duty with the Air Force, working on a special, top-secret project of joint interest to both the Army and the Air Force. In addition to working on the nuts and bolts of the joint venture as a G-2 air officer I, along with my Air Force counterpart, was to be in charge of all aerial phenomena. As fate would have it, that included what later came to be known as UFOs.

My introduction to UFOs was swift and unexpected. It came in the form of a telex (now called a fax) from headquarters. The telex was labeled "Top-Secret" and "Need-to-Know Only" and was a bombshell, for it completely changed my life and others' from that day on. The substance of that communication was that an Unidentified Flying Object (UFO) had soft-landed in the middle of one of the most, if not *the* most, highly classified and sensitive areas in the world, White Sands Proving Grounds in New Mexico, where we developed and exploded the first atomic bomb. Even today, the White Sands Missile Range remains among the most highly classified military sites in the United States.

I wish to impress upon you that the 1948 incident was not the first. In fact, it had been preceded by the Roswell incident which occurred in 1947 at Roswell, New Mexico. That incident, however, was accompanied by disaster. In the ensuing reclamation and retrieval operation, our government was able to recover only bits and pieces of the distressed ships (spacecraft) and their occupants. The Roswell incident is undoubtedly the most thoroughly researched and publicly documented episode of all UFO incidents. It is the centerpiece for the establishing of government interference and coverup of something that should have been declared openly to the public and then put under wraps for detailed study and contemplation. In fact, it was because of the government's cavalier and paranoid handling of this particular incident that the whole field of ufology has since then been so inappropriately handled on all levels.

One year after the Roswell incident, the White Sands incident occurred. Unlike the Roswell incident, it is still a ghost with little substance or credibility. Obviously, our friendly government had learned well from the Roswell incident, and since then, all extraterrestrial events have been the most closely guarded secrets, going beyond Top Secret. Nonetheless, here is a summary of the White Sands incident as I experienced it at the time.

The substance of the telex was that an unidentified object had soft-landed within the area of the White Sands Proving Grounds. It was currently under observation for signs of life and/or intentions. A cordon of security had been established around it. The rest of the message was too detailed to report here, but some highlights follow.

The ship was 100 feet in diameter and appeared to be a large probe or reconnaissance ship. It was shaped like a sphere; it was silver and made of a metallic-like substance unknown to our scientists. Five dead bodies were on board. All were diminutive in size with the largest being just under four feet tall. The other four were three and one half feet tall. All were humanoid, anatomically and physiognomically, but had some physical differences, apparently due to the process of atrophy. There were remnants of what once was a mouth; it was no longer mobile like that of a human. Obviously their form of communication was by other means, most likely telepathy. The same was true for their noses and ears, which also looked like remnants. Their heads were disproportionately large for their bodies, indicating great intelligence and cerebral dominance. There was no hair on any part of their bodies. Upon later examination, all bodies proved to be male but, again, their bodily features and organs were nonfunctional and in a state of atrophy.

Now that I have established some degree of credibility, let's bump the subject up a notch or two to degrees of understanding I have gained over the past twenty or more years since I've begun to research the subject seriously. I include these points to pique your interest and to challenge your range of understanding and acceptance.

1. UFOs are nothing new. They have always been here, for they are a presence in our collective and sometimes in our individual

consciousnesses. Biblical research finds no fewer than twelve occasions wherein the writer or commentator was obviously involved with an object of extraterrestrial origin. Some of the personalities involved are Ezekiel, Jonah, Moses, David and Elijah. Moreover, if one were to review the ancient Sumerian chronicles, man's first written history, one would find that they clearly state that men and vehicles of extraterrestrial origin put us here. Considering this and much more that could be added, it is unfathomable that governments and the majority of the world's population can deny the existence of UFOs and extraterrestrials and their interaction with our planet. It almost seems as though there is a conspiracy afoot to influence the man or woman on the street through subliminal conditioning to deny the existence of UFOs. And yet, oftentimes, normally censored information and reports appear. Why?

2. There are millions of people worldwide who have had personal encounters with UFOs or have extraterrestrially related experiences. These experiences include sightings, abductions and telepathic communications. In one particular incident that happened in 1991, a whole nation was put on alert when every man, woman and child, along with the full range of government officials, observed 60 extraterrestrial craft hovering over much of their country for 24 hours. No one was hurt or interfered with in any way. The country was Belgium. What was the purpose of the display of their existence and force in broad daylight?

Earlier, in 1950 during the Truman administration, 50 UFOs flew over Washington, D.C., and particularly over the White House, again for 24 hours. The *Washington Post* carried featured copy for one edition and then dropped it. Why? Why wasn't the rest of the country informed?

3. In a newspaper considered to be substandard like the *National Enquirer*, the *Globe* or the *Star*, there was a report from Bahrain, an emirate in the Persian Gulf area, that during the Gulf War, 52 UFOs hovered over the battlefield daily. Interesting! Obviously they were observers noting the conduct and outcome of the war. Were they the good guys or the bad ones?

4. This last question entertains an important point. Among us at this very moment are various and sundry extraterrestrial groups. Some are good, some are bad and others are neutral observers. The

first of the three types I call the Guardian Forces. They unequivocally have our best interests at heart but do not openly express such for that would represent undue influence which would be in violation of one of our most sacred and God-given gifts — free will. Instead, these forces influence us subliminally, registering in the form of harmonics and vibrations those things to which they hope we favorably respond. The special part of all of this is that through choice and free will, we can accept or deny the programmed desire or wish. It is our will that is done, not theirs. This is sacred, and they honor it. Some of us do favorably respond and then we become part of the Legions of Light.

The second class of beings are the "bad guys" who do not have our best interests at heart and are here basically to exploit us, violate our free will and use us to regain that which they have lost over the millennia — their humanity. To accomplish this, they have come among us to take forcibly what they need to create hybrid humans in the laboratories on their spaceships and on their home planets such as those of Arcturus and Orion. They have indiscriminately abducted human beings from Earth and removed vital parts and fluids from our physical and biological makeup, including blood, enzymes, body parts, semen from men, ovarian eggs from women, vaginal secretions, and sometimes even emotions.

It is questionable whether they can truly tamper with the soul. Certainly they cannot tamper with that most sacred aspect of our beingness which is that spark of divinity within that connects us directly to the source of all things and indeed is called God. Logically, if each of us remains in a state of Godliness and walks in love, Light and balance, we are immune to the incursions of these misled and aberrated beings. A word to the wise!

The third type are the neutral beings who are among us for observation and heaven only knows what other purposes in the future. Such speculations could range widely among possibilities that could eventually affect us favorably or unfavorably. From experience, I know some are basically reclusive and use our planet only as a terrestrial harbor while traveling between planets; they are resting and have no desire to interface with us. I feel that other observers are not to be trusted and are basically amoral, with little or no degree of compassion. I think they would squash us like bugs, if need be. Personally, I dislike this class of alien more than the second type of usurper who, even though they are out to use us and farm us, have made their intentions clear through their actions. What makes the observers sometimes even more beguiling is that they look so much like us, yet have the souls of the most demented and vicious biological beings. Through some of these very basic revelations you can see that the field of ufology is a complex one.

Although world governments have in some cases mastered some of the more advanced extraterrestrial technologies, particularly the building and successful flying of their own extraterrestrial vehicles, we are yet literally babes in the woods in comparison to the many who observe us and are actually among us.

Yes, they are here! We are all, terrestrial or extraterrestrial, a piece of the whole fabric, which incessantly begs to be unraveled in order that we may arrive at the truth. Unfortunately, the vast majority of people are too busy with personal pursuits to consider this subject and, consequently, add to the problem rather than helping to solve it. One of the surest ways to gain the truth is to walk and talk in love, Light and balance. When we do so, we attract the attention of the Guardian Forces which supplement and enhance our Godlike attributes and assist in the dispelling of the illusion we so freely but dangerously dwell in. Be one with God and all else will take care of itself, including the many complexities and illusions of ufology.

Why not? The bad guys are a part of the Creator God, too; but of course, this is a side we have yet to master and accept as a part of ourselves, that shadow side we do not want to admit we have, much less deal with.

I hope I have jostled your perhaps previously imperturbable rejection of UFOs, extraterrestrials and the little grey men that go bumpity-bump in the night. Of course, that was my intention, for sooner or later you have to get off square one and get involved. UFOs are real, and they have been here for millions of years. They are here now in great numbers to remind us that we do not belong here and that we, like they, also come from some far-off constellation that was once our point of origin. They are also aware that we are experiencing an uplifting of consciousness which could facilitate our ultimate and soul-felt desire to go home, just like E.T. did.

Happy transcendence, my friends. If you see E.T. on the way before I do, give him my best regards and tell him I, too, will ultimately be coming Home.

9

Astrology

Marilyn Waram

Astrology is the study of the relationship between planetary positions in the sky and human life and experience here on Earth. Astrology is many thousands of years old and appears in nearly all cultures in one form or another. People have long gazed up at the sky and wondered if the various objects up there had any significance for humans. Was there any meaning in the cycles and patterns? The consensus, now supported by statistical evidence, is yes; what goes on up there has something important to say about what goes on down here.

We see the correspondence between events in the sky and events here on Earth every day in such natural phenomena as the tides, the sunrise and sunset and the changing of the seasons. But astrology takes the association much further. Each planet is known to be related to distinctive character traits in human beings, as well as to specific types of events. This knowledge has been built up from observations over thousands of years.

A professional astrologer draws up a chart, or horoscope, for the exact moment in time that an event occurs. In the case of an individual, the natal chart is calculated for the instant of birth, usually taken to be the time of the first breath. The resulting chart shows the position of each planet at that moment. For reasons we don't fully understand, the start of anything, including the start of a human life, seems to be a moment of "imprinting."

The natal chart appears to show the dominant characteristics and traits that the individual will have throughout life.

Sun Sign Columns

Many people equate astrology with the Sun sign columns found in newspapers and magazines. These columns serve the purpose of introducing one basic idea in astrology to those who might be interested, but they are very simplistic. Professional astrologers make use of all the planets, not just the Sun. A human being is an extremely complex mixture of personality, habits and unconscious as well as conscious drives. The natal chart reflects this complexity with the planets, their signs and the actual area of the chart they occupy all having a particular meaning. Just like the often contradictory nature of humans, the chart may reveal several conflicting drives. It is this ability to see inner conflicts in the natal chart that makes astrologers so useful to those who seek to understand themselves better.

Every planet is important to an astrologer because each one gives different information. The Sun and the sign it is in are not always the dominant factor in a person's chart. That is why two people who have the same Sun sign may be quite different. For one person, the Sun sign may be dominant, whereas for another person, it could be an entirely different planet that is dominant.

Fate or Free Will?

There are two schools of thought in astrology. Do the planets in their various positions actually cause events to happen or indicate conditions under which certain events tend to happen? Those who believe that the planets, through some sort of ray or force, actually make things happen or predetermine a person's life, are stuck with another concept: fate. If the planets are in control, then we have little choice or power over our own lives.

The other school of thought holds that the planets are merely part of the evolving order of the universe. As such, they indicate the current (or past or future) state, rather like a complex cosmic clock, but they are participants in the process, not causes of it. This theory is far more empowering. It opens up the possibility that we do indeed have choices and alternatives. The planets then become symbols of our possibilities instead of dictators of our fate.

More Freedom Than We Know

Simple observation of human beings in action reveals that most of what is blamed on "fate" is simply the natural result of ingrained attitudes and habitual ways of behaving. Someone who is thought to be "lucky," for example, can be seen to behave in quite different ways from someone who is considered "unlucky." Sales managers are well aware that certain behaviors bring better results, so much so that they document those behaviors and attempt to teach them to their entire sales force. Personal-growth teachers also work on the premise that new behaviors and attitudes bring new and different results.

Those who are inspired by the idea of learning new behaviors, those who truly commit to new attitudes and beliefs, do bring about different circumstances for themselves, so it does seem that we can make choices if we are open to change. Yet curiously, those who do not adopt the proven way of succeeding will almost invariably blame fate or something other than their own behavior when they fail. Usually, however, they were simply not wholeheartedly willing to do what was required to succeed.

Often, people are not suited to a particular way of doing things. For example, quiet, retiring individuals generally do not feel comfortable using the tactics of high-pressure sales. Those tactics are too alien, too distasteful. If such people insist on trying to work as salespeople in a field that requires high-pressure sales, they will be miserable and they will tend to get poor results because they can't fully implement all the tactics or they get the timing wrong.

This doesn't mean they are "fated" to do poorly at sales. It means they will tend to resist or sabotage the behaviors that make for successful sales. But if they don't realize this, they will fail to see how their behavior differs from that of those who are successful and will look around for other reasons. They will, in other words, fail to see where they have choices and which choices led to the results they ended up with. Such people have a lot more freedom than they realize. Most people do.

Planets Show Tendencies

Astrology seems to reflect quite accurately this state of affairs. What horoscopes reveal about people and situations are tendencies, not absolute certainties. People can and do change. They learn to manage their tendencies: they learn to temper automatic reactions, to take a deep breath and do what they know will bring the best results. But if they act without thought, the chart will describe what their automatic tendencies are.

As mentioned earlier, each planet is associated with certain behaviors. The planets that are strongest in a person's chart depict that individual's strongest tendencies. The sign each planet occupies describes how the person acts on those tendencies. For example, the Sun is associated with self-worth and those issues about which a person needs to feel proud. The placement of the Sun in the chart gives strong clues about how the individual gains attention and respect. The Sun in a retiring sign such as Pisces indicates people who have trouble getting noticed strictly for themselves. They usually try to get attention indirectly, either for acting like someone else or for their artistic or healing abilities. The Sun in an outgoing sign such as Sagittarius, on the other hand, usually indicates someone who has no trouble asking for what he/she needs. Consequently, unless there are strong indications otherwise in the chart, Sun in Sagittarius is usually associated with someone who has a good sense of self-worth. It works the same for all the other planets.

Fire, Earth, Air and Water

The planets generally answer the question "what?" The signs, on the other hand, usually describe "how?" As we saw above, the Sun relates to self-worth, while the sign the Sun is in tells how the Sun needs are usually met. Each sign has its own traditional way of behaving. Each planet is more compatible with some signs and less comfortable in others. A quick way of determining whether a particular sign helps or hinders the goals of a given planet is to use the categories Fire, Earth, Air and Water.

Fire is the element of "positive" emotions such as excitement, enthusiasm, confidence and optimism. Fire signs all have these qualities in common. The Fire signs are Aries, Leo and Sagittarius. The Fire planets are Mars, the Sun and Jupiter.

Earth is the element of pragmatism and "husbandry," or taking care of things. It is methodical. The Earth signs are Taurus, Virgo and Capricorn. The Earth planets are Venus and Saturn.

Air is the element of thought. It is rational and logical. The Air signs are Gemini, Libra and Aquarius. The Air planets are Mercury and Uranus.

Water is the element of deep feelings, including those arising from the unconscious. It is emotional and sensitive. The Water signs are Cancer, Scorpio and Pisces. The Water planets are Moon, Pluto and Neptune.

Generally, Fire gets along well with Air. That is, Fire planets are comfortable in either Fire signs or Air signs. They are restricted by Earth or Water signs. Earth and Water are compatible. Earth planets are comfortable in Earth or Water signs but find Fire or Air signs too jarring and alien.

The Meanings of the Planets

The planets describe what is done.

Mars: that part of human nature which naturally asserts itself and its own desires; associated with high energy level, anger and fighting.

Venus: that part of human nature which naturally attracts what is desired; associated with artistic ability, love of comfort and ease.

Mercury: the logical, rational conscious mind; associated with information-gathering, paperwork, brothers and sisters and dexterity.

Moon: the mothering, nurturing part of human nature; emotions, strong family attachments, shrewdness in business, sensitivity and moodiness; associated with the mother.

Sun: self-worth and self-esteem; need for attention, need to be able to have an impact on the world; associated with ego, charisma, creativity and willingness to take risks.

Pluto: the "shadow" side of the unconscious; all the powerful urges and drives that civilized humans find hard to accept in themselves; associated with intense emotions, power, sex, death and elimination.

Jupiter: the capacity for faith and trust; associated with beliefs, values, ethics and morals, but sometimes also with a curious double standard — the rules may apply to others but not to self.

Saturn: a sense of responsibility, productivity and the ability to cope with the demands of reality and society; associated with father, discipline, law (natural and man-made), conscience and fears.

Uranus: the urge to become an individual, to be unique and different; associated with rebellion, avant garde thinking and innovation.

Neptune: the deepest spiritual essence; associated with unconscious beliefs, artistic ability, spiritual healing and psychic ability.

Meanings of the Signs

The signs describe ways of doing things.

Aries: enthusiastic, impatient, restless, quick, fond of new experiences.

Taurus: stable, security-oriented, fond of beauty and comfort.

Gemini: curious, intellectual, a collector and spreader of information.

Cancer: nurturing, sensitive, clannish, shrewd.

Leo: dramatic, proud, a natural leader, actor, teacher.

Virgo: work-oriented, analytical, quick to see flaws, reserved.

Libra: people-oriented, social, gracious, a natural networker.

Scorpio: powerfully emotional, intense, possessive, secretive, passionate, masterful.

Sagittarius: confident, exuberant, optimistic, a pursuer of knowledge.

Capricorn: work and productivity-oriented, highly responsible, one who needs to be in control, one who has Puritan ethics.

Aquarius: social, intellectual, radical, individualistic, one who lives on his own terms.

Pisces: emotional, vulnerable, spiritual, mystical.

Other Pieces in the Puzzle

Planets are located not only in a particular sign, but also in a house. A house is the name given to a section of the chart. The chart is usually divided into twelve houses, each with its own meaning. In addition, the distances between the planets are measured, with some set distances being called "aspects." For example, if two planets are 60 degrees apart, they are said to be "sextile" to each other. Aspects yield yet more information about how the various inner drives either cooperate or conflict.

Besides the planets, many astrologers add asteroids to the chart. There are also various astronomical points and points derived from complex formulae, all having particular meaning.

Putting the Pieces Together

It is up to the astrologer to take all the detailed bits of information available from the chart and make some sense out of them. This process is called "synthesis," and it is generally acknowledged that it is one of the more difficult tasks for the human brain to learn. Astrologers have varying degrees of mastery of synthesis; some have natural ability, others have had good training and have improved through practice. Without synthesis, an astrological chart is just a kaleidoscope of bits and pieces. With it, the chart becomes a dynamic descriptive map of an individual human.

The first step in synthesis is to isolate one planet and consider what it might mean when that planet is in a particular sign. For example, does Mars act the same when it is in Leo as when it is in Pisces? The analysis of elements shows immediately that a Fire planet such as Mars is going to be more comfortable in the Fire sign, and less comfortable in the inward-turning Water sign of Pisces. Water tends to hold energy in. So it is possible to form a simple hypothesis based on this information: Mars is probably more outgoing and energetic in Leo and less outgoing and energetic in Pisces. Mars is likely to be much more easily able to ask for or take what it wants in Leo. In Pisces, there is a strong possibility that Mars will be held in, possibly to the point of being repressed. This process of isolating one planet and considering its meaning only in relation to its sign position or only in relation to its house position or in its aspect to one other planet is called delineation. Often one planet's delineation will describe a personality trait that is in complete conflict with another planet's delineation. Such a condition describes an inner conflict which the individual may not even be aware of. A good astrologer must be able to delineate every factor in the chart, then take a leap into synthesis. From there she/he must be able to translate the information into easy-to-understand language, so that the individual can follow the interpretation and gain a much deeper understanding of his or her own tendencies and talents, strengths and challenges.

What Can an Astrological Interpretation Reveal?

Depending on the experience, background and skill of the astrologer, a good reading should identify an individual's most productive career path(s) and his or her most satisfying type of relationship as well as compatible traits to look for in a partner. It should reveal inner conflicts that may be sabotaging conscious goals and help the client understand how to handle the conflict constructively. It should reveal talents such as artistic or healing abilities, the capacity to be highly organized or to be good at research. A chart interpretation can usually uncover the major life issues for a client and can show how those issues operate on the spiritual and psychological levels as well as on emotional and physical levels.

One of the most electrifying experience for a client is to have an astrologer draw a clear connection between some life pattern that keeps repeating (such as failure at work or in relationships) and a belief that is held at the unconscious level. Once a client understands the meaning behind the outward pattern, he/she is often in a position to "get off the merry-go-round." That is, with insight into why he has gotten into a pattern in the past, he can choose healthier ways of dealing with his inner conflict in the future.

A comprehensive chart interpretation can look back at the client's relationship with his/her mother and father and reveal whether issues left over from those relationships are likely to color and perhaps wound current relationships, especially with one's love partner and children. There is information about the most satisfying leisure pursuits as well as how much in control a client needs to be. Although the chart does not reveal specific details, it does point out the issues quite clearly. How the client deals with those issues is where freedom of choice comes in. The chart contains fascinating information on nearly every subject, far too much to impart in a single reading. However, an experienced astrologer can pick out the most important themes and explain those clearly, giving the client much insight, even in an initial interpretation. Also, most clients come to a reading with specific problems on their minds, and they may prefer to discuss those problems in depth rather than to cover other less immediate issues. To a certain extent, then, what a chart reading reveals depends on the skill of the astrologer and the needs of the client.

Finding a Good Astrologer

It is probably clear by now that an effective astrologer, one who helps clients understand how to change their behaviors, needs a background not only in astrology but also in counseling or psychology, preferably both. Astrologers who confine themselves to world events do not need to worry about such training, but it is vital to those who work with people. Much harm can be done by an astrologer if she/he draws a negative conclusion and then tactlessly presents that conclusion to a client. Astrologers have their own biases and human frailties. Some take the time to become more aware of their own issues and problems, and they learn how not to let their personal issues cloud the interpretations they give clients.

There is no over-all governing body in the field of astrology, although some organizations do offer certification. If an astrologer has gained a diploma, it at least indicates that she/he was willing to work hard to learn astrology to a certain level of competence. Lack of a diploma, however, is essentially meaningless. Some of the best astrologers have worked very hard to learn their subject, have studied with various teachers and attended conferences, yet have no desire to align themselves with one school or another. Consequently, they have no certification. One way to tell these astrologers apart from dabblers is by word-of-mouth referral. Good astrologers have a high rate of client satisfaction.

It is also possible to ask an astrologer questions about his or her approach and background. For the merely curious client, level of experience is probably not too important, but if serious problems are at issue, a well-educated professional astrologer should be chosen.

The first place to look for an astrologer is in nearby metaphysical bookstores. They often have one on staff or they know of several and what their specialties are. Astrologers are usually interested in other metaphysical disciplines as well, so local psychic organizations might be a good source, too. In larger cities, there may be magazines and newsletters in which astrologers advertize. A bookstore can often provide these. And finally, some astrologers do list themselves in the yellow pages.

Do-it-yourself Astrology

Delineating a chart requires access to tables that list planetary positions and aspects. A bookstore that carries such references and tables usually also carries what are called "cookbooks." These are books that have written delineations for each planet position, sign, house and aspect. It is possible and even fun to look these up for a particular birth date and refer back to the delineation. They will often give a surprising amount of information and insight.

There are also computer charts available, complete with a written analysis. Some of these are very high-quality. However, like the do-it-yourself method, synthesis is lacking. Consequently, some of the information will be conflicting and may be misleading.

For a good analysis, it is worth it to pay for the services of an experienced professional astrologer. Some astrologers do interpretations over the phone or on cassette tape so that people in isolated areas can still get a high-quality reading.

If you are interested in learning more about astrology, start by reading. Stay away from most Sun sign books and shop in metaphysical bookstores. Well-written astrological texts are of no interest to the general public so they do not appear on the shelves of most bookstores. Staff at the metaphysical stores can usually guide you to the best reference tables and books. They may even offer or know of classes that are available.

Astrologers today avidly study psychology, counseling skills, mythology and statistics, among other disciplines. They bring their new knowledge back to astrology, enlivening it tremendously, and deepening the understanding of all practitioners who keep in touch. Astrology is a living, growing, dynamic discipline.

For many people, astrology is a hobby that they pursue for their own understanding and pleasure. It is a hobby that offers fascinating new insights into human nature for as long as it is studied.

Recommended Reading

Arroyo, Stephen. *Astrology, Psychology and The Four Elements.* Sebastopol, CA: CRCSP Publications, 1975.

March, Marion D. and McEvers, Joan, *The Only Way to Learn Astrology,* Vol. I. San Diego, CA: ACS Publications, 1976.

Oken, Alan. *Complete Astrology.* New York: Bantam, 1988.

10

Numerology

Lynn Buess, M.A., Ed.S.

Fundamentals of the Chart

In preparing the individual numerological chart, each letter in the name is assigned a numerical value. The total values are then

1. computed for the full name;
2. computed for the vowels and consonants separately.
3. Each total is then reduced to a single digit.

The letters a, e, i, o, u, and y are calculated as vowels. (There is some debate among numerologists about y, but after years of research, I now always compute y as a vowel.)

The numerological correlations for letters in the alphabet are as follows:

1	2	3	4	5	6	7	8	9
A	B	C	D	E	F	G	H	I
J	K	L	M	N	O	P	Q	R
S	T	U	V	W	X	Y	Z	

Following is an example of finding the numbers for an individual name:

	J A M E S	E A R L	S M I T H	
Add:	1 1 4 5 1	5 1 9 3	1 4 9 2 8	Total = 54 = 9
Add:	1 5	5 1	9	Vowels = 21 = 3
Add:	1 4 1	9 3	1 4 2 8	Consonants = 33 = 6

	M A R Y	(no middle name)	J O N E S			
	4 1 9 7		1 6 5 5 1			T(otal) = 39 = 12 = 3
Add:	1 7		6 5			V(owels) = 19 = 10 = 1
Add:	4 9		1 5 1			C(onsonants) = 20 = 2

The calculation is based upon each person's full name at birth — first, middle and last. In the case of "Jr.," "IV," etc., the name is calculated as follows:

J OH N P A X T ON FI T T S WOR T H J UN I OR
1 6 8 5 7 1 6 2 6 5 6 9 2 2 1 5 6 9 6 8 1 3 5 9 6 9   or

J OH N P A X T ON FI T T S WOR T H T HE FOUR T H

This is done even though the birth certificate may be written "JOHN PAXTON FITTSWORTH, Jr." or "JOHN PAXTON FITTSWORTH IV." When there are two or more middle names, they are all computed.

Below is an example of two names that will assist you in computing a comparison chart:

M A R Y   E L I Z A B E T H   H O P'E F U L Y
4 1 9 7   5 3 9 8 1 2 5 2 8   8 6 7 5 6 3 3 7   T = 109 = 10 = 1
  1   7   5   9   1   5   6   5   3   7   V = 49 = 13 = 4
4   9   3   8   2   2 8   8   7   6   3   C = 60 = 6

R O B E R T   F R A N C E S   W U R E E D
9 6 2 5 9 2   6 9 1 5 3 5 1   5 3 9 5 5 4   T = 94 = 13 = 4
  6   5   1   5   3   5 5   V = 30 = 3
9   2   9 2   6 9   5 3   1   5   9   4   C = 64 = 10 = 1

MARY with ROBERT

T = 1	T = 4	= 1 – 4
V = 4	V = 3	= 3 – 4
C = 6	C = 1	= 1 – 6

The Human Cycle

Numbers symbolically outline the path of human involution and evolution. We are going to examine the meaning and symbology of numbers with slightly new guidelines and perspectives. The following key interpretations shed light upon some archetypal meanings inherent in the structure of numbers:

When zero, or the *full circle*, is used it represents the higher self or superconscious. It is the capacity to move awareness to a higher plane for perception.

The *straight line* represents conscious awareness. The vertical line is masculine and assertive in its action. The horizontal is feminine and receptive.

The *crescent* represents the soul or in some cases the subconscious. It is receptive to information or subtle energies and rebroadcasts them on the conscious level.

With these fundamental keys in mind, we can pursue the anthropogeny of numbers. The fourth wave of divine sparks represents three-faceted atoms poured forth from the body of the solar logos and periodically inspired by cosmic stimulus. They are like virgin spirits with the threefold nature of deity incorporated as their essential dynamics. Yet despite the simplicity of deity they possess, the sparks lack awakening to full awareness of their divine attributes. To gain this, they start on a voyage of the universe, plunging into the various strata and planes of matter to educate themselves and become masters of their universe. This voyage eventually includes passage through the planes of each of the planets in the solar system.

The sparks descend through the highest spiritual planes and the monad, or higher self, becomes self-conscious on the third plane down. The sparks then attach themselves to the personality which includes substance from the three lower planes. With the mind as a link between the higher levels and lower levels, the human being begins to build the soul consciousness. Through rebirth and reincarnation into many personalities over time, the soul consciousness evolves under the tutelage of the higher self. It employs the vehicles of personality for opportunity to grow in mastery. The soul develops with accumulation of the experiences garnered through embodiment. Through guidance from the divine spark (the higher self), the soul endeavors to balance excesses and avoidance in experience and to bring all events into mastery. This has been a brief outline of the chain; how this chain of events is revealed through numbers follows.

The number one in the human cycle represents the divine spark still at one within the embracing realm of the solar logos. Total consciousness prevails and life is in harmony with all beings in the body of god (the solar logos, not the absolute).

With the number two, we have the fall of man. Soul awareness begins to awaken, and the consciousness of the lower self is in a receptive phase of development. The lower planes here receive the archetypal format that molds the vehicles for use by the soul and higher self.

With three, we see the soul adjusting to awareness of both the spirit realm and the material realm. Here it seeks a balance to bring spirit and matter together. This phase also is indicative of the division of consciousness into male and female forms. It inspires the seeking of unity and balance by working consciously with a mate to bring forth life and creative expression.

Four reminds us of the threefold consciousness taking on the form of body. Man stands upright now with the germ of his divine self awaiting the trials of Earth for unfoldment. The cross epitomizes those trials and sacrifices to come. It is the number of form and of Earth.

In number five the consciousness of senses and mind reigns over the soul. Five is the number of experience, free will and lessons to be learned through indulgence in the lower vehicles. It leads to awakening. It is the number of man.

Having encountered multitudes of lifetimes and experiences, the realization grows that maybe there is purpose to life. Man begins to take responsibility for his action; he vaguely seeks the higher self which is still at the bottom or in a dormant state. The thrust is now upward.

The number seven represents mastery and balance over the lower levels. The male-female (yang-yin) energies are in a harmonious flow of intuitive receptivity and assertive action. Wisdom is attained and the aspirant now begins to direct attention to higher law.

Counterpoint to seven, showing mastery and

balance of the Earth plane, eight shows the rhythm and balance of eternity. The aspirant here attunes to the law of spirit and executes it all the way through his or her life. Higher law prevails in Heaven and on Earth. Eight is authority and brings leadership and divine administration.

Nine is the number of the New Age. It is the divine man on Earth. The superconscious is now predominant, and its directives flow to Earth. It is attainment and fulfillment of perfection on the Earth sojourn.

These are certainly only capsule summaries of the potential in the numbers. The reader is encouraged to spend additional time on inner study and in meditation upon these ideas to best deepen his/her understanding of these stages in unfoldment.

Another brief sketch may provide more clarity to the searching mind. The flow of the numbers reveals the descent of the divine spark into involvement with matter; with its awakening and ascent or evolution, we move to divine consciousness.

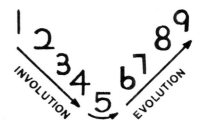

Students have often raised a very significant question at this point in the study. Why move from pure spiritual existence into material existence simply to return to spirit? This crucial question plagued my early years of study. This answer represents the best of my understanding at this point in consciousness — subject to change upon illumination!

Our true identity is that of a divine spark. The divine spark issues forth from the body of God and is a three-faceted replica of its creator. The divine spark has awareness of a divine simplicity but none yet of the universe. It attracts atoms from each level to form an awareness on all seven levels. Through eons and sequential spirals of lives, the personality and soul are finally mastered; the experiences from these attributes of self are impressed upon the divine spark. At the end of the evolutionary spiral on the planet, the divine spark emerges with divine consciousness plus self-consciousness. The divine spark is intimately linked to the traveling atom, so we are a part of that consciousness.

Once the entire circumstances of this planet have been mastered, the cycle is repeated on the other planets until the whole systemic circumstance is completed. Then the developing deity may work with the solar logos for its internship of divine preparation. Perhaps it works with the will activity, then the wisdom, then the love action.

Having graduated from systemic mastery, the lesser deity may work for yet another great entity in another galaxy. Finally, the mission is complete. The traveling atom, having completed all the planes and rays, begins to orbit a greater sun and projects its own thought form into space to become a creator (great entity) in its own right! "Know ye not that ye are Gods?"

My feeling at this time is that the wave of divine sparks today involves millions of the Earth's human population still living in unawakened mass consciousness. Many are on the verge of self-awakening into individualized consciousness of personality, and a few of soul. Other awakened souls serving as teachers and advanced students of Light are, in most cases, beings who have come to the Earth from another planet to contribute certain teachings and complete specific karmic lessons.

By studying the name and birth date chosen in this lifetime, each of us has a guideline to certain potentials, pitfalls and opportunities we will encounter. By wise application of this knowledge, growth can be accelerated and destiny attained with greater ease. Numerology can shed more light upon your search for self. It can help you to reach mastery of this particular Earth spiral in your environment.

The Vibrational Aspects of One to Nine

Our whole world of living is one of responding to vibrational patterns or creating them. These patterns can be discordant or harmonious. Each of the bodies in our seven levels of consciousness works within a specific range of vibration. The planets, the sun, our Earth and all its life — each has its own vibration. Through the interaction, stress and reconciliation of these various patterns, we evolve.

Each number has its own particular aspect or vibrational characteristics. There are three principal tendencies inherent in each number: the assertive (yang-masculine); the passive (yin-feminine);

and the harmonious (equilibrium). An examination of these principal tendencies in numbers follows.

1 — Individuality (Will)

Assertive: willful, domineering, selfish, arrogant; one who puts own needs before others' regardless of personal consequences; boastful, impulsive.

Passive: dependent, submissive, fearful of making decisions or taking initiative, stubborn, procrastinating.

Harmonious: strong-willed and ambitious, considerate of others, courageous, an organizer-leader-pioneer, individual, original thinker. For the one to find a point of balance between its own extremes, it must learn to resonate with the number two, whose primary lesson is:

2 — Cooperation (Peace)

Assertive: meddling, arbitrary, careless, strident, tactless, extremist, dishonest; one who overlooks detail, creates divisiveness.

Passive: vacillating, sullen, devious, fault-finding; one who pays too much attention to detail, causing delay in accomplishment; unable to take a stand.

Harmonious: diplomatic, adaptable, able to fuse divergent opinions or groups, rhythmic, gentle; one who gathers information from both sides of a position before taking a stand.

The two can get caught between other viewpoints and needs and therefore, to establish balance, must learn to resonate with the number three, whose primary lesson is:

3 — Self-Expression (Creativity)

Assertive: superficial, extravagant; one who likes to gossip, has false vanity, a wasteful ego, an attachment to creative gifts, gaudy taste; not fond of the practical.

Passive: one who lacks concentration; fails to fully develop creative potential; asexual, gloomy, lacking in imagination.

Harmonious: gifted with fluid speech, creative and artistic, intuitive, joyful, sociable, enthusiastic, tasteful in dress and decorum.

The creative expression of number three may go undeveloped or can take on such an exaggerated spontaneous execution that it is too out of the ordinary for the acceptance of the intended recipients. To balance and properly express talents, the three needs to resonate with the number four, whose primary quality is:

4 — Discipline (Work)

Assertive: stubborn, intolerant, too serious, brusque, lacking in emotional sensitivity; one who overworks and sees only one way of doing things.

Passive: lazy, resistant to new methods, narrow; one who must see practicality before accepting ideas; fights intellectualism.

Harmonious: loyal, consistent, patient; one who fulfills a given task well, sticks to facts, has integrity; organized, economical.

The tendency of fours is laziness or too much repetitive activity in the method of approaching life tasks. "All work and no play makes Johnny a dull boy," so fours need to resonate with the number five, whose primary lesson is:

5 — Freedom (Change)

Assertive: restless, irresponsible, nervous, over-indulgent (particularly with senses); one who has too many interests, ignores rules and laws and disregards values.

Passive: afraid of the new, of change, desirous of a rule for every behavior; sexually confused, unable to learn from experience, uncertain.

Harmonious: progressive, diversified in terms of talents and friends, curious, a freedom-seeker; quick, flexible, adventurous, energetic; a traveler.

Fives tend to overindulge in experience or fear experience and move along too quickly without learning the meaning of an experience. Fives seek perspective and balance from the six:

6 — Responsibility (Service)

Assertive: over-involved with others' problems, self-righteous; worrisome, domestically dictatorial, prone to arguing, overly conventional, easily upset.

Passive: one who martyrs himself, resents service, lacks concern for family and home; a constant complainer, anxious; one who carries too many burdens (real or not) on his/her shoulders.

Harmonious: unselfish, artistic in taste, conscientious, fair; one who seeks emotional equilibrium in self and others, has a harmonious home, serves humanity.

Sixes either take responsibility too seriously or avoid it like a plague. They are often victims of their own emotional imbalance who can best find an antidote to their flaws by seeking the qualities of the seven, primarily:

7 — Wisdom (Detachment)

Assertive: severely critical, too analytical, intellectually conceited and vain; deceptive, aloof, eccentric, faultfinding.

Passive: skeptical, cynical, suppressive, cold; crafty, prone to emotional withdrawal, secretive; one who has an inferiority complex and thinks rather than acts.

Harmonious: an excellent analyst; one who seeks deeper truths, has technical ability, reaches, has faith; mystical and intuitive if higher mind is tapped; stoic of temperament, discerning, poised.

Sevens have a tendency to become overly attached to unintellectual viewpoints, or they may fear mind-development and new ideas. They must learn to put ideas to practical use through administration and execution with proper use of the eight vibration:

8 — Authority (Power)

Assertive: over-ambitious in order to attain leadership or power; callous in his disregard for others, crassly materialistic, one who demands recognition, loves display; abusive.

Passive: fearful of failure, unable to take a leader's role, poor in judgment; scheming, disrespectful of authority, dishonest in business, careless in regard to money.

Harmonious: one who has executive ability, respects wealth, administrates with personal consideration for others; successful, a good judge of character, confident.

Eights fear or misuse power and money. An unenlightened eight uses others to gain selfish ends and can create much suffering for others. Eights work best to balance their extremes by learning particularly from the nine:

9 — Altruism (Compassion)

Assertive: impractical, fickle, over-idealistic; one who lacks toler-

ance for others' views; too generous, indiscreet; anarchistic, in ex-
treme cases.

Passive: aimless, gullible, easily used by others, depressed, indif-
ferent, pessimistic about the world and the future.

Harmonious: inspired, attuned to New Age concepts, compas-
sionate, generous, gifted artistically; a perfectionist; one who works
to build group consciousness and seeks world brotherhood and harmony.

Nines can lose themselves in broad ideals and group or universal
causes. Their desire is great to let go of self to serve the selfless calls
of the New Age. They need to balance the potential loss of self-iden-
tity through attunement to the vibration of number one, individuality.

A Word About Master Numbers

Some authors of numerology identify the numbers 11, 22 and 33 as
master numbers. From my research and personal experience, I feel
that there is a definite added potential and vibration to these numbers.

A frequent misassociation with master numbers is that they are an
indication that the person is a master from the planetary leadership of
ascended souls (the Hierarchy) who has incarnated. Or there is a
tendency to think of a person with a master number as an awesome
leader who holds in consciousness some magical powers and metaphysical mystique, but this is seldom fully true.

It is possible that one or more of the hierarchical souls may choose
to incarnate for a special purpose, and their names or dates of birth
may possess master numbers, but by no means can we expect everyone born with these numbers to be such souls.

In most cases, however, the presence of master numbers does
suggest an older soul coming into this lifetime to make an important
contribution for mankind in a field of a spiritual, scientific, medical,
religious, educational, governmental or technological nature.

Often, master numbers indicate an older soul trained in the ancient
esoteric schools many lifetimes ago who now returns to manifest or
teach particular New Age methods of healing, psychic development or
invention.

In rare instances the presence of master numbers may indicate a
dynamic soul who is incarnating this time from another planet or

system to fulfill some specific destiny or mission.

Many old, important and masterful souls have names and birth dates with no master numbers, so we must be careful to keep this whole matter in perspective.

My studies have brought me to the tentative conclusion that no matter where the master number may appear, the higher vibration does not fully unfold until the soul has awakened. In many instances certain gifts manifest through grace; in fact, the individual possessing the gift may not have initiated conscious discipline and study of spiritual law in this lifetime.

Those who have master numbers appearing in their names or birth dates generally are endowed with special tendencies toward leadership and inspiration that set them apart from mass consciousness. Because the numbers are of intensified vibration and potency, those who possess them have a heightened obligation in life, such as greater requirements of self-discipline and purification of consciousness.

Until the needed purification and awakening of soul awareness take place, the individual operates in the vibrational influence of the two rather than the 11; the four, rather than the 22; and the six, rather than the 33.

Tendencies and qualities exhibited by the master numbers follow.

11 – Revelation

Assertive: fanatical, cultic, overzealous; one who lacks practical realities, attacks dissimilar viewpoints, uses psychic or divine gifts for self-purpose.

Passive: apathetic, sensitive to public reaction; one who fails to apply inspiration, over-reacts to criticism, fears higher energies and gifts.

Harmonious: inventive, a visionary leader, a gifted channel or clairvoyant; one who seeks to express higher consciousness, unites spiritual truth to the material plane.

Elevens fly high in the clouds and must strive to plant their dreams on terra firma. To effectively convince others and stimulate change in the world, elevens need to study and absorb the quality of the twenty-two:

22 — Sacred Structuralization

Assertive: one who tends to over-evaluate self-importance; exaggerates information, promotes hasty causes, resents lack of recognition, misuses wisdom or power.

Passive: apathetic toward human needs; unable to adapt self to group needs; in extremes, one who uses heightened awareness for criminal goals or black magic.

Harmonious: in control of self and environment, one who integrates higher wisdom into organizational administration, one who puts universal goals ahead of self-pride; a practical mystic.

Twenty-twos become so engrossed in the work of their destiny and mission that they fail to recognize the subtle emotional needs of coworkers. In their labors, they often forget the human quotient, so they benefit from learning the lesson of the thirty-three:

33 — Universal Service

Assertive: — forceful in attempts to serve others, intolerant of differing mores and opinions, over-emotional, unable to adjust to needs of others.

Passive: overprotective, rebellious; one who hides from positions of responsibility, seeks praise, backs down from own position to have harmony.

Harmonious:— sympathetic, a good counselor (often psychic or spiritual), a kind of cosmic parent or guardian; one who has concern for the welfare of the masses, creates harmony at home and at work.

Thirty-threes in many instances have an ego need to demonstrate just how hard they are working to serve others. It creates a grandiose martyr complex when unchecked. They benefit from the idealism of 11 and the intellectual practicality of 22 to keep the magnitude of their work in perspective.

What You Choose to Receive from Life

The most significant interpretations in the natal chart are the birth date and the breakdown of the name as it was at birth. From the name comes insight into one's character, potentials and weaknesses, with numerous shades of self-evaluation. Now we will consider the significance of the birth date.

The date of birth is determined by the soul and higher self of the incoming child. Every mother has the experience of knowing that when the child is ready, birth occurs. It is right and proper that the soul do the choosing, because the life number indicates the type of circumstance, opportunities, challenges and destiny that life experience will bring to the soul for experiential evolution. The life number provides a clue as to what fate has in store. How one will react to life depends upon the numbers in one's name, one's own free will and one's attitude toward encounters with life's events. Proper utilization of numerological guidelines can provide each individual with tools of consciousness. If the tools are handled with skill, each person can better understand self and life. With understanding comes the foundation upon which effective actions are based; and right action releases us from the wheel of karma and rebirth, furthering the evolution of the soul onto higher spirals and planes.

The Life Number

Now it is time to see exactly how the life number is ascertained. The life number is derived from the sum total of the numbers in the month, the day and the year of birth which are reduced to a single digit (except when dealing with master numbers).

For example the birth date of July 21, 1931, is calculated as follows:

$$7 \quad 21 \quad 1931 \quad = \quad 7+2+1+1+9+3+1 \quad = \quad 24$$
$$= \quad 2+4 \quad = \quad 6$$

$$\begin{array}{ccc} (7) & (3) & (5) \end{array}$$
or: $\quad 7 \quad 21 \quad 1931 \quad = \quad (15) \quad = \quad 1+5 \quad = \quad 6$

Another example is November 12, 1934

$$11 \quad 12 \quad 1934 \quad = \quad 1+1+1+2+1+9+3+4 =$$

$$\begin{array}{ccc} (11) & (3) & (8) \end{array}$$
or: $\quad 11 \quad 12 \quad 1934 \quad = \quad 22$

In the above instance, the sum is 22 and since it is a master number, it is not reduced to four. When 11's, or 22's appear in the month, day or year, they are generally left in that form for purposes of calculation.

One more example: January 10, 1908

$$\begin{array}{ccccc} 1 & 10 & 1908 & = & 1+1+0+1+9+0+8 & = & 20 \\ & & & = & 2+0 & = & 2 \end{array}$$

$$\begin{array}{ccc} (1) & (1) & (9) \\ \text{or:} \quad 1 & 10 & 1908 \end{array} \quad = \quad (11) \; = 11$$

In this example, the number 11 does not result in one of the two examples given. Since it is there in one, the 11 vibration has to be considered as a possible influence. The strength of influence must be weighed from an examination of the entire chart.

11

The Tarot

Marlene Ayers-Johnston

Reading Tarot cards is the art of fortune telling. The deck of cards is made especially for this purpose. It tells about the past, present and future as well as about spiritual, psychic and material attributes. There is no end to the aspects the Tarot can reflect. There is a quote from the Svetasvatan Upanishad that says, "Thou are man, thou art woman, thou art boy, thou art girl, thou art an old man tottering on his stick." Human beings can be all of these things in one day or even in one hour, according to what the challenges or rewards are at the moment.

The Tarot is believed by some to have come from the ancient Egyptians. Others believe the Chinese created this masterpiece or perhaps the Gypsies brought it from India. There may also be some truth to the conjecture that the Tarot came from the harems of ancient Arabia.

Ultimately, it doesn't matter where Tarot cards came from; what does matter is that anyone can use them. The more you learn about tarot, the more you want to learn, especially once you develop a feel for the cards and start doing readings.

The Tarot can be used for fortune telling but to limit it in such a way would be to debase its transcendent significance. "Know thyself" continues to be a valid dictum, and the Tarot can reflect the hidden truths of the self. An intelligent use of the Tarot for divination will provide valuable guidance in the mundane events of life and give a fair indication of likely trends in your undertakings. There is no element of fatalism in this, for no matter what course the Tarot may indicate, your free will controls the final decision. Each situation or problem in life always has at least ten options. The Tarot can help to explore those options, indicating avenues previously unconsidered.

The Major Arcana and the Minor Arcana

The Tarot deck is made up of 78 cards which are divided into the Major Arcana and the Minor Arcana. The Major Arcana consists of 22 cards representing aspects of the human soul such as greed, isolation, love, abundance, power, fate and death.

The Minor Arcana is made up of the remaining 56 cards which are divided into four suits: Wands, Swords, Pentacles and Cups. These cards can also be representative of a regular deck of cards: the Wands represent clubs (Fire); the Cups, hearts (Water); the Pentacles, diamonds (Earth); and the Swords, spades (Air). These cards can represent the more mundane aspects of your life.

Wands have always been my favorite of the Minor Arcana's suits. They represent change, ideas, creation, animation, energy, wisdom from past lives and, last but not least, agriculture. Wands can also reflect the fair-complexioned person with blond or auburn hair and blue eyes. There are other things they can represent and there will also be the meanings that you will attach to them. It is important to make the readings yours and to make them personal for the client.

Swords generally represent the quest, aggression, ambition, boldness, force and courage. They can also mean transformation, hate or war if they are associated with certain other cards. There can also be constructive and destructive aspects, friction, defense and striving associated with these cards. Sword people may have dull complexions, dark brown hair and grey or hazel eyes.

Pentacles, or coins, as some people call them, consist of circles surrounding five-pointed stars made of intersecting triangles. Generally, they point to matters connected with money, material gain or attainment on the financial plane. They may also refer to development, trade and industry. In Medieval times pentacles were seals or metal discs inscribed with various magical formulas. Five-pointed stars are the time-honored symbol of the magical artisan. They also represent the five senses of man, the five elements of nature and the five extremities of the human body. The Pentacle person can have a swarthy complexion, dark brown or black hair and dark eyes. He or she can be a very intense, deep person, not as much on the surface and out in the open as the Cup person or the Wand person.

Cups generally indicate good news, love and happiness, or the lack thereof. They express the good life — fertility, beauty and the emotions, rather than the intellect. The sign refers to water, symbol of love, instruction, pleasure and knowledge. Cups can also indicate alcoholism or the out-pouring of emotion. Cup people look rather watery, with fair complexions, fair or light brown hair and eyes of grey or blue.

The Minor Arcana is numbered one through ten, with the Page, Knight, Queen and King in all four suits. I have put into my deck the Maidens, which reflect young women up to their mid-twenties. The Maidens were taken out of the deck in the twelfth century when witchcraft and witch hunts became so prevalent. The Pages reflect young men (twelve and under) or messengers. The Pages can also reflect the person being read for when he was under the age of twelve. The Knights reflect young men from the age of about twelve to thirty-five. The King then takes over, reflecting men over thirty-five. Queens take over at the mid-twenties and continue beyond.

I have also inserted into my deck a question-mark card. This card appears when the questioner's answer will come at a later date, if it is to be answered at all. Almost all Tarot decks come with extra cards expressly for the purpose of adding your own personality to the deck.

Other Meanings

It is important to study the cards. I don't mean to get all the books that you can find and read up on them, I mean to look at the colors on the cards, to look at the figures, observe which way are they looking, walking, standing or sitting. All of these things are important and can have much meaning.

The left side of the card is usually thought of as the past and the right side as the future. You can also consider the left side of the card as female and the right side as male. There will be further meanings that you attach to different cards as you perfect your style and references. As you become familiar with the cards, you will find methods and meanings that work for you and for the subjects for whom you read.

The colors hold almost as much importance as the characters on the cards. Yellow can represent the mind, mental abilities; orange can represent humor and the hidden agenda; green can mean healing, money or jealousy; red is energy, anger or sexuality.

The numbers on the cards also have very important meanings. Most of this is basic numerology. Whatever the numbers reflect to you, consistency is the true key when reading the Tarot. Here are a few of the many meanings for the numbers:

0 – Roots/the beginning – all or nothing.

1 – Individuality/the self – strong or weak

2 – Choices/money, material possessions – partnerships or opposition

3 – Intellect/communication – support systems or habits (good or bad)

4 – Structure/Mother Earth – a base to grow on or being stuck in one spot

5 – Creativity/lovers – talent or acquisition of things or people

6 – Changes/action/health/daily work

7 – Unseen spirits – partners or marriage

8 – Transformation/other people's money

9 – Cycles/higher learning – a new path or repeat lessons

10 – Status in the community or chosen profession – concerns or opportunities; can indicate being Earthbound

11 – Friends/intense relationships

22 – Karma/intensely intense relationships

There are also instances when the numbers on the card are added together, such as adding the one and the two in 12 to come up with a three. You are now watching the colors on the cards, the positions of the cards, the numbers on the cards, the characters and scenes depicted and the cards in relation to each other.

You also have the option of taking into consideration the reversed position. Cards in the reversed position can change the meaning of the card completely, although in some instances, which only the reader can determine, it does not affect the meaning.

There are many layouts that can be used for a reading. Try all of them and see which one works best for you. Then again, you may find you like to do different spreads for different people. Each deck has examples of spreads in the pamphlet contained in the package, with complete instructions about how to lay the cards down and indications of their individual meanings. Each person brings to the reading his or her own intention, clarity and interpretation.

Procedures

To begin a reading, quiet yourself, light a candle, say a prayer for clarity and centeredness and pick up the cards. Bless the deck, yourself and the person you are doing the reading for. Some people don't want anyone touching their cards, so they do all the shuffling, laying out and cutting of the cards. Others prefer to let the person being read for hold the cards, concentrating deeply on the question or problem while shuffling the deck. The client can shuffle for as long as he wants to; then he divides the deck into three separate piles, using his nondominate hand. The reader then restacks the cards and begins the reading.

If you are shuffling the cards, it is important to keep your mind focused upon the question to be answered. If, while shuffling, you are thinking about something mundane such as picking up a loaf of bread or having the oil changed in the car, it will show in the cards, and the layout will be confusing and not reflect your question clearly. The Tarot can be a perfect reflection of what is going on in your life — deep spiritual reflection or the most mundane.

There is an aspect of Tarot reading that cannot be written about: a card turned up during a reading indicates one of two persons — either the person asking the question or someone in that person's life. It may be someone from the past, present or future. This matter can be resolved only at an actual sitting with a qualified reader. Readings can easily be slanted in different directions. The first two cards turned over will tell about the subject of the reading or about the question being asked. Only the reader or the person asking the question can determine what the cards are representing. To attempt to tell you exactly how to do a reading in this limited space would be folly on my part.

I have not mentioned the individual cards because they are all reflected and interpreted in the brochure that comes with the deck. I believe that your imagination will give you the meaning of the cards, reflections that are held in your soul. These meanings are the most significant. That is why it is important for you to get your own deck and read for yourself. Be your own source of divination. Tap into the infinite wisdom of the universe, that wisdom which is your soul.

The Tarot cards like to be kept in a natural environment. That keeps the energy from becoming scattered or intruded upon. Wood provides a good natural environment and is used by many. Others prefer silk. A silk bag seems to set the mood for that very special moment.

Conclusion

Plato was quoted as saying, "Thou art the stormy cloud, the seas, the seasons. Thou art without beginning. Thou art infinite, thou, from whom proceed all universes." We are all those things. "...After having attained [your] health and integrity, recover the luminous path of [your] pristine state." Here, Plato meant that once we are aware of our obstacles and our dreams are defined, anything is possible.

The Tarot can aid in seeing into the depths of the soul. You can obtain a clearer understanding of your true nature by reading the cards which can serve as pointers to what lies concealed below the surface of the waking consciousness. The cards can reflect and help to reveal weakness or prejudices, dreams you never knew you had and fears from beyond this lifetime that can keep you from living your dreams. Rightly used, the Tarot can perform the function of a psychotherapeutic agent.

We are limited in achieving our dreams only by our imaginations, and today we are learning to develop our imaginations more and more.

Recommended Reading

David, Karen J. *I've Got Your Number!* New York: Bantam, 1992.
Gray, Eden. *A Complete Guide to the Tarot.* New York: Bantam, 1983.
Waite, Arthur Edward. *A Pictorial Key to the Tarot.* New York: Carol Publishing Group, 1979.

12

Palmistry

Marlene Ayers-Johnston

Palm-reading is one of the most fascinating arts you can enter into. There are no special tools needed, no special books or gimmicks, just the willingness to concentrate, pay close attention and learn. It doesn't even take a lot of time to learn to read palms, and there is always one around when you have the desire to study.

One caution I will give you is that there are people who are just starting to move into higher consciousness and awareness. If while reading someone's palm, you jump into deep esoteric or spiritual levels, you may upset him or her. He/she may not be looking for such information at the time; that will have to be determined by you, the palm-reader, by observing the person's body language.

There is certain responsibility in doing palm-reading or any other reading, for that matter. If someone asks a specific question, then make it a point to answer that question, even though it sometimes seems that a person would rather not know. You can phrase the answer in such a way that the person feels he is making his own decisions.

Reading People

Before you begin to read palms, you learn to read people, and that includes their entire personas. The most expressive (and unconscious) thing about a person is his body language. This was the "secret" of the most successful palm-readers in ancient times. True, there is the art and the science of reading the palm, but there is also an art to knowing how much to reveal and when in the reading it should be revealed.

Pay attention to how your subject is holding his or her hands: close to the face (perhaps wanting to say something or holding something back; with open palms (open-minded or "nobody home"); thumbs stuck into the palm and covered (very low self-esteem). These things will tell you about your subject before you even pick up the hand. Sometimes you will know all you need to know without even looking into the hand.

How the hands are held tells you about the emotional state of the subject. Watch how freely the arms swing. What are the hands doing when the person is relaxed? Are the hands fluttering around while he talks, indicating an expressive person, perhaps a person who exaggerates? Hands have a "mind" all their own. Most people are totally unconscious of their hands and how those hands are busily expression all of their thoughts, hopes, fears and feelings.

The appearance of the hands can change overnight. It is important to photocopy both hands once a year to observe the changes that are taking place. The spaces between the fingers can change in terms of how you hold your hands. The fingertips can change; they may bend in or bend out. The position of the thumbs can change radically. The skin texture can also change. You may get red spots or white spots. They are readable too, especially as you become more aware of how you fit into the universe around you. Red spots in a certain part of the hand mean that something is going to happen in that particular area.

Another thing to observe is how people wear their jewelry. The client can make a definite statement with jewelry. Are rings simple or fancy? Are they worn on every finger or is there one carefully placed ring? On which fingers are the rings worn? Rings could be a complete chapter unto themselves.

There is also the body posture to consider such as stooped shoulders or hiding the eyes with lots of hair (not wanting anyone to notice him or see who he really is).

There is no great secret. Just pay attention to people and their actions and reactions to other people and situations. Become an observer.

Cautionary Comments

When you are reading a palm, the person may be uncomfortable with what you are saying. If the person crosses his arms or legs or avoids eye contact, go no further with what you were telling him, and change the direction of the reading. It is important to soften the reading or, if you are about to hit a nerve, keep it on a nonthreatening level or go on to another area of the palm. If you really have some burning information that needs to be conveyed to your subject, it may be worked into the reading a little later, after you have ascertained it is something they absolutely must hear. It is my complete and utter belief that it is not your business or right to tell all that you see or feel in a person's hand, and it is a reader's responsibility to avoid giving a person more information than he can handle. It is vital to gauge the person and see just where he is in his awareness.

It is important to use phrases like "tendency toward" instead of saying, "You will be doing drugs" or "You will be involved with someone who does drugs." Instead, you could say, "You may come in contact with someone who does drugs."

People usually don't know what they are asking for when they say, "Look at my palm and tell me what you see." You must judge what information they are ready to hear, and what it is he or she wants to know. "Am I going to get that raise?" "Is my son ever going to finish college?" "Am I going to live through this?" "Is this person I am in a relationship with going to be the one for me?" These are all very different types of questions. Some people don't really want to know the truth; most people just want to hear that everything is going to be fine. It could be wise to study psychology before learning palmistry. The importance of knowing your subject as well as your subject matter cannot be strongly enough stressed.

The Hand Itself

On the physical level, you are going to read the size of the hands in proportion to the body, the shape of the hand, the palm of the hand and the fingers. Pay attention also to the temperature of the hand. Is it warm or cold? A warm hand might mean the person is not comfortable.

One of the first things to consider is the shape, proportion and flexibility of the hand.

The square palm with fingers about the same length as the palm is the hand of the practical or physical person. These people are usually level-headed, fair-minded, orderly, sometimes tenacious and hard-working.

The elementary hand is short and thick, with stubby fingers and a nail formation with little shape. These people can be slow thinkers and have an indifference to anything but their immediate needs. They are usually guided by their instincts.

The psychic hand is slim with long tapered fingers usually having pointed tips. These people are vulnerable and tend to have gentle, idealistic personalities. They are not forceful. They are sometimes unworldly and easily hurt because it is easy to influence them and take advantage of their gentle natures. These people are usually interested in the arts and the unseen and the frequently display psychic talents. They use their minds to solve problems.

The conical or artistic hand is full and well-shaped. The fingers are tapered. These people, if not in the arts themselves as creators, have a strong appreciation for the arts. They are good companions, usually easygoing, enthusiastic and dynamic. They are generous, do not take well to regimentation and are happier working on their own, doing what they want to do when and in the way that they want to do it.

Then there is the philosophic hand. It is angular and long, with pronounced joints on long fingers. These people have a sense of dignity and sensitivity, are deep thinkers and can sometimes be misunderstood by others.

The Fingers

The fingers themselves are most informative. For instance, the index finger is the Jupiter finger. This is the finger of judgment and personal achievement.

The left side of the body is the self, the female side and the past. If one injures his left index finger with a hammer while wishing he hadn't just told his spouse to get off his case, this is an obvious example of too much self-judgment. A scar on the index finger, left side, would indicate an almost terminal case of self-judgment that has become a permanent part of the personality. If one injures his right index finger with a hammer while wishing he hadn't just told his spouse to get off his case, this would indicate one who wishes he had said a whole lot more but suppressed it instead.

The middle finger is the Saturn finger. It is also called the God finger because of lessons learned easily or the hard way. If one hit his middle finger, right hand, with a hammer, it would be a nonverbal way of saying, "This smack is for you."

The next finger is the Sun finger, or the ring finger. When the Saturn finger and Sun finger are very close together, it indicates that a person has a very good understanding of who he is and of his place in the universe, that he feels at one with the Creator.

There is also the mixed hand which can be a combination of all the above: short fingers with a long palm or stubby fingers with a very slender, delicate palm. There are never two exactly alike.

The Palm

The mind has many dimensions. As it thinks in pictures, it is causing electrical impulses. The electrical impulses cause action. As one uses one's hands to touch, to feel, to act, one's movements are being recorded; the brain is a computer. If two impulses are on the same nerve and they meet, that causes a resistance. This resistance causes depressions, or lines, to form on the hands. This is how the lines are formed and this how they change.

The hand one writes with is the predominate hand. This hand is read first. It is the hand of the present and the future. The other hand is the hand of the past and of possibilities. Lines will develop in the nonpredominate hand and transfer over to the other hand.

Now we shall talk about lines. Deep lines reflect a lot of energy. The deepest lines are usually the life line, the heart line and the head line.

The life line starts somewhere between the first finger and the thumb and curves around the thumb. It tells how one is going to live one's life and indicates one's vitality and longevity, although it does not tell exactly how long one will live. Look at the depth of the line, interruptions in the line and other lines crossing it. A short life line can say that the subject may be greatly influenced by other people, not living his own life and can also likely be influenced by his surroundings.

The head line cuts across the center of the palm. A deep head line would tend to indicate a person who makes up his own mind and is not easily swayed. He may also have a very strong intellect with lots of mental activity. If the head line has lines that cross over it or if it is broken, then there is mental confusion and mental interference. A short head line would indicate that there is not much interest in learning.

If the head line and the life line are connected, the basic tendency is to feel first, to be very emotional and then to think and analyze later. If there is a gap between the head line and the life line, the person may analyze first and then feel. The bigger the gap between the head line and the life line, the more analytical a thinker is before you. A bigger gap still and you have the abstract thinker, the logical mind that can perceive things no one else can and that has an interest in scientific things.

The heart line, running across the hand closest to the fingers, can show physical problems, how one loves and how love comes to a person. The person with a deep heart line loves deeply and has a strong set of values. The heart line relates to values — people, possessions and ideals.

Now that we are in the 1990's, new lines are showing up in people's palms. These lines are not explained or reflected many in books as yet. There are also new groupings of lines that have just recently started appearing. The laws of humankind no longer apply. We are limited only by our consciousness and our imaginations. Now we know that if we can imagine something and put it into our consciousness, it can happen. We are creating it. There is no longer the need to create little wars (or big ones) to raise our awareness. There is no longer the need to create illness, trauma or drama in our lives in order to change the direction in which we are going. We now know that we have free will and consciousness.

Palms in the 90's are also showing that we are much more active in our so-called "golden years," and we are creating more of an impact in our later years, not just living longer. We are truly growing older and wiser.

In olden times certain lines had very definite meanings. That is no longer the case, now that we know we have free will and a higher consciousness. It is part of the spiritual revolution and evolution — the evolution of the more intuitive person. The prophecies in "The

Revelation" go only as far as the year 2000. I believe that this is because people have not been conscious that they have been creating their own realities — and their own miracles — on a daily basis.

As you become a palm-reader and a reader of people, you will develop your own style and system and flow. Take your own sweet time. Develop your style.

There is so much more to say about palmistry. Only a small speck of information has been covered here, so investigate your bookstores and libraries.

Recommended Reading

Benham, William B. *The Benham Book of Palmistry.* North Hollywood, CA: Newcastle Publishing, 1988.

Gettings, Fred. *Palmistry Made Easy.* North Hollywood, CA: Wilshire, 1977.

Squire, Elizabeth Daniels. *Fortune in Your Hand.* New York: NAL-Dutton, 1978.

Wilson, Joyce. *The Complete Book of Palmistry.* New York: Bantam, 1983.

13

Earth Changes Create Body Changes

Speaks of Many Truths through Robert Shapiro
June 1993

Τhis is Speaks of Many Truths. Earth changes are creating physical changes in your bodies right now. Mother Earth has ordained herself, aligned herself and attuned herself to her immediate present-future. Now how can something be both future and immediate?

As you know, something can happen now, for example, striking a cymbal, and yet the vibration and some of the ring goes into the future as well. But this attunement is different. This attunement has been brought about by the cymbal's being struck in the future and the unfoldment of time has allowed Mother Earth, in her cycle, to begin to reach the vibration of that tone. You, being guests on Mother Earth during this time, have signed on as crew for this journey and have no choice, really, but to fall under the same influence.

Flowing into the Attunement

So this is suggestive, is it not? If the attunement was "waiting for you" and you are now just flowing like a ship into the harbor where the attunement is waiting, then who has set up that attunement? Was it Mother Earth herself? Yes, in a sense. Certainly it was the Creator, and yet it was also your own souls. Long ago, before your incarnational cycle that included the Earth, your souls set up a time with a little flexibility.

That attunement would happen even if you had not begun shifting into the higher achievement of yourself. The attunement you're coming into right now is a safety net that would have caught you had you and Earth been ponderously, sluggishly toiling along toward the old destiny which would have been considerably more unpleasant. But that is not the case, so it means that you can move more swiftly now that the attunement is pulling you into the harbor of your own consciousness.

Some of you experience a vibration in your solar plexus from time to time and have noticed this increasingly for the past few months. This is part of it. Mother Earth's solar plexus would be equal roughly to her medial crust, essentially two-thirds of the way out from the center of herself. Here she is experiencing a vibration from time to time. This vibration is designed to change the very matter of her substance.

Needless to say, as a result it is going to change the very matter of your substance. It's going to add very slowly certain etheric components that exist in possibility and probability and that also exist within the encompassed objectives of your soul's journey through this place, the Creator's playing field. It's going to mix these etheric components in and out of your physical body, the way you would dunk a tea bag into hot water.

The effects are very jarring in some ways. On the one hand you'll get physical vibrations that are strange and sometimes feel uncomfortable. Sometimes your endocrine system will speed up or slow down, causing various effects on your hormones. Sometimes you will have a sudden strong feeling and then, snap, it'll be gone. Other times, you'll have an overwhelming memory and you will not be certain whether it is a memory or a dream. It will seem so real it will be very difficult to tell whether it is a dream or a reality.

So, this kind of expansion in consciousness is literally pulling you into worlds that are beyond potential and are becoming real. Things about your world are changing in front of your very eyes. Perhaps the most profound change is the need that many of you have noticed lately for more rest. Anybody feeling tired lately? All right. Lots of response there. Your body systems are overloaded, in a sense. Mother Earth's systems are overloaded, too. Her body, the mass of herself, functions very much like your own. How many people know that Mother Earth breathes, actually breathes in and out? That's right. People who have been in caves or have been near the openings into the Earth can actually hear that air whistling in and out. But as the result of underground work, mining, explosions, changes, a lot of her breathing holes have been restricted or even blocked completely.

Some people think that Mother Earth breathes through her volcanoes, but that's not really true. She births through her volcanoes. She can, as a last resort, breathe through them, but it's not an easy thing to do. You could breathe through your ears if you absolutely had to; the doctors could make a passage, but you would never be the same again.

So, it is this: You are tired all the time because she is tired. She can't catch her breath. And many of you feel that you can't catch your breath. So she sleeps, deeply, but it is not a sleep that achieves rest. How many of you wake up in the morning and still feel just as tired as when you went to bed? The same is true for Mother Earth. She will rest, in her seasons, one side of her in the winter, the other in the summer. Winter is her slumber, but she hasn't been getting good rest. Come springtime, not all of her energy is available, so not all of the plants, not all of the animals, not all of the people have the energy they need.

All of your energy, without exception, comes from Mother Earth's energy field, her auric field; that is, the physical component, not the spiritual component, not the spark of life given by the Creator.

How to Help Raise the Energy Level of Mother Earth

Her energy body is low now. If you were able to perceive from space — some of you can see by distance viewing or in meditation — you would see that there are patches and holes, thin spots, areas where her auric field is weak. If you were to hold a person up next to Mother Earth's energy body and blow him up to about the same size, you would see, in roughly the same spaces, holes and places where the energy is being drained or where there is not enough energy. Mother Earth cannot spare enough from her own energy body to give your energy bodies the substances they need to function perfectly.

What I am suggesting here is that there is not enough time to repair, rock by rock, stick by stick, the changes that have been wrought in your age of technology, so you will all have to do something besides that. This is going to allow you to use your capacities. You have heard of a car falling on a man and a woman unthinkingly lifting up the car and pulling him out.

When there is a crisis, you tend to forget your limits. When there is a crisis, people forget their differences and rally around. These limits are largely self-imposed, but some of them are imposed in such a way as to allow you to experience new ways of creating and resolving all of the dilemmas.

But now Mother Earth needs your help. You have more than a vested interest in giving her this help. Consider this homework; we will practice it here. Some time in the next three months, take a solid hour of your time. If you don't have the energy for that, then you can take smaller blocks of time, but this has to be done in perfect sequence. If it's a half hour, it has to be at noon this day and noon the next day. It has to be sequential. Noon is chosen because the sun is high in the sky. There's a little more balance then. You have a little more support for your energy when the sun is high in the sky.

This is what to do. I'm going to ask you to imagine that there is an emergency. Just imagine yourself being in a desperate emergency and reach beyond the present. Reach into the future with one hand, reach into the past with the other hand. Let your energy reach up to the sun and down on the other side of the Earth to the moon. Pull into the center of you, into your heart, all of the physical light, love, rainbows, the essence of beauty, all that is timeless that is you, the creator. Pull into your heart all of the beautiful energy that you have ever been and say that out loud: "Please give me now all of the beautiful energy I have ever been, just for this time." It will come into your heart and it will be more than you need. What will happen is that it will naturally radiate to Mother Earth.

Just focus on that energy for that hour of time, if you can hold it, or half hour, or ten minutes, or five minutes, but always at the same time and on sequential days for a total of no more than sixty minutes. You will help her, all of you who are here, and all of you who read this, in whatever language and form you hear of it. It will be greatly appreciated by Mother Earth and, of course, appreciated by you, as well. Alter all, do you really think, for example, that the ozone layer is going to be fixed by something mankind does with technology? It will be fixed by something all people do with their hearts, with their spirits, with their prayers.

Now, I'd like you all to practice this for a moment together so as to feel a sense of unity. When I say the word, I want you to reach into the past, reach into the future, reach up to the moon, reach down to the sun (or vice versa) and then pull in as much of the beauty as you can. I want you then to say out loud or under your breath, "I ask that all of the beautiful energy that I am come to me right now for me to experience so that the excess can flow into Earth Mother." Now.

That's good. Relax. That's very good. Now you know what to do.

Mother Earth needs your assistance and you need hers. The reason you are tired is that she is tired. The issue here is urgent. Many of you have heard the scientific reports that the oxygen in your air has greatly reduced itself. On the one hand we can say oxygen is something that will not be in your future as far as what you will breath. Nevertheless, your physical body is made up to need it right now, and, in order for you to experience your full capacity of energy, you need more oxygen. So here's some extra-credit homework for those of you who like such things.

Reseed the World

Some time, again in the next three months, get yourself a tree seedling; go out and plant it. Water it enough so that it will be able to catch and get into the ground...if not on your own land, then somewhere out in the countryside. If there is no countryside, plant it wherever you can, but plant something green. The plankton are becoming less active and all of the oxygen-giving lifeforms are less present or less active — that's another scientific reason you don't have much energy. Nevertheless, Mother Earth has the capacity to reseed the world. She must feel that you want it to be done. In recent years, she has been urging her trees to show you that it can be done. She has been urging her plants, her plant friends, if you like, to show you that reseeding can be done. Some of you have gotten the message the wrong way and have had lots of children, but all right. Nevertheless, it is also important for you to reseed the plants whom you give life by what you exhale, who give you life by what they exhale. Mother Earth wants to show you what can be done.

Your breath, as I said, has been affected. How about your hearts? We know that they're being speeded up energetically in order to allow you to infuse more of your true heart energy, which is located not only in your physical body, but in your etheric body as well. On the one hand, you could say you're speeding up your vibration in order to experience your true selves. Yes, that's so. On the other hand, for some of you this is creating heart challenges.

The issue here is that for some people it will be necessary to level your energies. By leveling them I mean to embrace the Earth. How does one embrace the Earth? It's kind of hard to stretch your arms around the Earth, but you can stretch your arms around a rock and you can feel yourself becoming the Earth. Anybody who has heart challenges, become the Earth. Do a meditation. Do a prayer. Have an experience where you feel yourself becoming the stone, becoming the water. This way you will help your heart.

Here's a little extra thing. For those of you who are near the sea, the rhythm of the tides is geared not to breath, but to heartbeat. As the waves flow in, they are geared to heartbeat. If those of you who have heart challenges can go to the ocean, don't just count the waves, but feel yourself in the water, feel yourself a part of the wave. That will help the rhythm of your heart.

Many of you are experiencing challenges such as dietary anomalies. Some days you feel as though you could eat your way from one end of the supermarket to the other. Other days you feel that food is totally boring and why would anybody be interested in it. Mother Earth is changing her diet now. Yes, Mother Earth eats. She doesn't eat the same things you do but she eats. Mother Earth consumes, recycles and regenerates her atmosphere. When she has a volcanic blast, she throws bits and pieces of herself up into the atmosphere. You call it sulfur ash, but Mother Earth actually needs to have a certain amount of her own self-generated ash in the atmosphere. Not a lot, but some, all the time. She has to consume some of that oxygen for her fires.

She has to exhale certain gases, some of them so rare that they actually are not listed on the periodic table of Earth's elements. They're not listed yet because they're inside of her body, locked in there for safe-keeping. But in the next three to four years, she will be releasing from her North Pole, from her South Pole and from fissures created by earthquakes and volcanoes. She will be releasing gases, rare earth and elements that have never been to the surface of the Earth since Earth has existed.

Mother Earth's Regenerative Self Is Sealed Within

Mother Earth was simply an erupting ball of fire when she was birthing herself from the cosmic cloud that existed here before her existence. She sealed her regenerative self inside of herself. This is a key point. It is sealed from all forms of attack both purposeful and unintentional. An example of an unintentional attack would be when somebody, an oil company perhaps, fires ultrasonic waves into the Earth looking for oil or gas. That ultrasonic wave goes right through the Earth, very often. That would be an unintentional attack. An intentional attack might come from some potentially malevolent source that would like to see the Earth evolve in a different way.

Mother Earth has her regenerative self inside of her. This means that she has the physical matter, not just the spirit matter, not the cosmic matter alone, but the actual physical matter that it takes to set up the catalytic changes on her surface and in her subsurface and in her caverns and in her atmosphere to rebirth herself. If she released it all, all life as you know it would come to an end on the surface. But she is prepared to release enough so that it comes to the surface, percolating deep beneath the dry lakes, coming up as a form of gas, creating what some geologists will say smells like a combination of ozone and sulfur. They'll be concerned with the area if it is volcanic; it may be, but it most likely it will not be. She will create fissures if she needs to bring more gas up into her atmosphere.

Her whole point is to regenerate herself quickly but cause the least loss of life. This is suggestive, if you consider it. You are made up of Mother Earth's body. Even the physical substance of your auric field is made up of Mother Earth's body. This means that you, yourself, have located within you matter equal to her own. The regenerative self is not the soul. We know that the soul exists throughout all time and carries with it the essence of the Creator's personality as it wishes to reincarnate with you. Nevertheless, Mother Earth, being a miniature version of the Creator, as all life is, has her own version of the regenerative self or, essentially, a soul.

Mother Earth's soul is a spirit, yes, but she is a physical, material master, so she must have a substance that is equal to her spirit, something that can be felt, generated and regenerated. Because it is her job to demonstrate material mastery to you, she must have the substance of it. You, being little versions of Mother Earth, have the substance of it, too. This is a very important point. It means that Mother Earth will regenerate herself, releasing these unknown elements, elements that cannot unite. You can try to shove certain elements together, but they don't go together. She will create ways in which they will go together. If they are needed to bring about the change, they will immediately reform inside of her, about five miles down. She will refissure herself. She will recave and recavern herself. She will recreate herself physically.

What does this mean to you? Where is your recreative, physical sell? It is located in the lining of that which is referred to as your navel, your bellybutton. Where it connects to your mother, it comes into your body and it continues on a little bit, though it's tied off. If you could see it scientifically, it actually goes in a little further, not much but a little further. Your regenerative self is located there physically. It has the capacity to release elements that are unknown in the human body. It has the capacity to revamp your entire immune system. It has the capacity to change your lungs, your heart, your blood, everything, so that you no longer need as much oxygen, and so that you will be comfortable in the atmosphere you are easing into while you are alive, what you're calling the fourth dimension, but what is actually kind of a temporary place before you jump into the fifth dimension pretty quickly.

This regenerative physical self has already been activated. That's the main reason you're so tired. There's a revolution going on in all of your bodies right now. There are substances racing around in your bloodstream. Your white cells don't know what to do. Sometimes they are attacking these substances, and yet when they attack these substances, it is as if your white cells themselves are being raised to a higher level of consciousness. As a result, within three years, the immune systems of your bodies will be able to deal with substances that exist in the fourth and fifth dimensions which you will have to be able to deal with.

Indications of Diseases Will Occur Way in Advance

It will also give the children who are born for about the past two months and from now on the capacity to be very quick to be able to resolve certain preconditions of diseases. Right now there are certain diseases that have such a subtle warning that you usually don't know that you've got it until sometimes it's too late, or until it's done a lot of damage. But what will happen in the children and what you yourselves, no matter how old you are, are evolving into now, is that the preconditions will reveal themselves much sooner. It's as if your immune system, instead of becoming tired and worn down because it needs oxygen, will become sharpened up and will live off the impurities that you have ingested, breathed in, or been exposed to in one way or another. In a sense it's as if you're becoming a nuclear furnace that can burn anything that has an atomic structure. An advanced version of a fusion furnace can do this. You're really becoming that.

So as a result, the experience of your immune system is going to change. Instead of subtle messages that are often misunderstood such as "oh, you've got a cold," or "you've got allergies," you'll have alarm systems that go off so that you will know of it before you get some devastating illness. In the future, before a devastating illness such as cancer, you'll have symptomology, not of the disease itself, but of a phantom version of the disease. You might get a sudden lump. It's there, it catches your attention. In three days, it's gone, but it has caught your attention. This will warn you that your body will develop cancer within 20 years. Isn't it wonderful that doctors can have a 20-year headstart? By the year 2000, you'll have so many genetic medicines out and available, if not in this country, then in other countries, that they will be essentially inoculating people against devastating diseases.

So our immune systems are becoming more sensitive, not less sensitive, and you can be prepared for that so that when you see things, you don't just slough them off and say, "Oh well, it disappeared, great! Forget it." It's important now to communicate with your healers, your doctors, whoever you go to for healing. For you out in the countryside, maybe it's shamans, huh? That's what we did in our time. You'd say, "Shaman, I had a lump the other day but it's gone." And shaman says, "Oh, we'll take that spirit out right now." It works for us, but that's another story.

What about allergies? Why do so many people have them? For one thing, Mother Earth is encouraging reseeding. In the future you will need certain plants that have been extinct for years. Sometimes these plants go so far back that they existed in prehistoric times, and the only way to get them to the surface is through earthquakes, Mother Earth bringing up those gases with pollens and seeds floating up with them. Or — dare I say it? — yes, it's true, here's where technology is inadvertently assisting. People digging down in construction projects

are giving everybody major allergies because that dust they're bringing up has pollen and seeds from ancient life. They will create plants
that you have not seen for a long time, plants that are essentially
fossilized. Now comes the time when the botanists, the anthropolo-
gists and the archaeologists come together to form a new profession
based upon all three sciences. In many cases, the archaeologists will
know more about the ancient plants than the botanists themselves.
So Mother Earth is looking out for you. She is bringing things to her
surface in her own ways and you, inadvertently, are helping her. This
is not to give you license to dig holes and throw dirt up in your air.
But it's happening.

Prehistoric Healing Plants to Re-emerge

There are plants that existed in prehistoric times that can cure
every single disease that you have in existence today, as well as
diseases that you haven't even seen yet. Of course, that brings up the
question, "If pollens and seeds are coming up out of these holes what
else is coming up? Is it possible germs are coming up too?" You bet.
So that's another reason there is an alarm bell going off. This is
Mother Earth's system of communication.

Mother Earth is a good mother. Even when she has to take care of
herself, she is looking out for you. There will be new diseases based
largely upon what is called pollution. The plants that you have not
seen for quite a while will be reborn to treat diseases you haven't seen
for quite a while. But don't be frightened. Most of these diseases you
haven't seen for quite a while will take ten or twelve years to come
around, and the plants will be with you before then. They'll get a lot
of attention. As I said before, they'll be quite a surprise. "What's this
doing here? I haven't seen you since my last trip to the museum and
then you were pressed in a rock." Quite an interesting time to be a
botanist. Quite interesting.

Now let me anticipate one of your questions. Someone is bound to
ask, "What good thing is in my bellybutton, and how can I make it
work faster and better?" It'll work fine at its own speed. If you really
feel the need to stimulate it a bit, don't stick your fingers in your
bellybutton. On the bottoms of your feet, just a little bit in from the
midpoint of the arch, is a point you can massage as deeply as you can
comfortably deal with. That will help. In general I recommend foot

massages. It might be a good time for such a thing.

If the ozone depletion has led to an increase in skin cancer, what Earth changes correspond to the spread of AIDS?

Good question. Earth changes aren't the cause but why has it spread so rapidly? I will rule out the culprits, all right? I won't pursue that angle. The fact that the disease is a syndrome suggests that the immune system cannot deal with the conditions it is exposed to. I will not support the idea that the organism that has been isolated causes AIDS. It does not. I repeat, it does not! What would be Mother Earth's version of the immune system?

Her energy?

Her wind. Mother Earth's wind has been kind of restless. I'm going to include in wind cyclones, hurricanes, tornadoes, all of that. In some cases for strictly peaceful purposes and other cases for not-so-peaceful purposes, a lot of people have been messing with the weather. This has been for economic reasons in some cases, and for less altruistic purposes elsewhere. That has to change, because Mother Earth's wind then must respond. If Mother Earth and her wind were not messed with, you wouldn't have so many devastating tornadoes and hurricanes. But it is being messed with. So, the thing to be done is to recognize that every time anybody drops even one little crystal of silver iodide into the clouds to cause rain, it also affects the wind. This has been going on militarily and economically for the past 40 years.

What would be the Earth changes corresponding to tuberculosis or the new disease that is similar?

That is also associated with the wind but it is associated with the water as well. I don't have to go into what has been going on with your water, but Mother Earth is actually working on that one. I guess she has to melt the polar ice caps a little bit because of other things she needs to do with that water. It's not going to be a catastrophic melt, but a little bit. She's working on that.

But remember what is going on. Material is being brought up from the inside of the Earth. It's not a problem when it comes up volcanically because in that case it's purified. When it comes up simply through greed, that can bring up difficulties. I will say that this "new" disease is an old disease, just like many of them, that was dealt with about 100,000 years ago, maybe closer to a quarter million years ago, and was no longer a factor.   It's been brought up by excavation.

What was the antidote to that disease at that time?

At that time, there was a major fire. Not quite worldwide, but years ago when Mother Earth had to create a cauterizing situation, she would do what she does now: she would use her lightning, and fires would burn for long, long times. No fire engines then. That's what caused the cure. The plants producing that particular disease were almost totally eliminated.

What is the antidote?

The closest thing to an antidote now is oxygen therapy. Those therapies are not widely available in this country but they are more available in other countries. So physicians, explore oxygen therapies. This does not mean atmospheres that people breathe. It will be more like generating oxygen reactions in the lungs, in the bloodstream. We're talking about using not liquid oxygen, because that's actually a substance you have now, but a form of more densified oxygen. It is not actually breathed into the lungs but may be injected in the area.

Would hot mineral springs also provide that benefit?

We're talking about this specific disease. If those mineral springs are hot because of genuine volcanic activity, meaning within a 150-mile radius of a volcano, maybe.

What about the hydrogen peroxide therapies?

I don't think that would be directly helpful for this specific disease.

Could you tell me if it could he used for other things?

Possibly.

Are the lungs (and lung diseases) related to fear?

Since the lungs are active in breath, the fear is something that's being breathed in. Where is it coming from? Is Mother Earth fearful? Well, you know, that's an interesting thing. Mother Earth does not actually have fear. But you know something? That which you call fear is not really fear of other, it is a level of instinct that is designed to protect and preserve. So since Mother Earth is involved in emergency protection and preserving of her life, one could say it is fear energy that is being breathed in. But Mother Earth does not have fear as you know it. Neither do you, but we're not going to be splitting hairs. She does have a high level of activity going on to support her urgent needs, so in actuality, you are breathing that in every day.

In regard to the new plants that you were talking about, I had a fossilized rock in my front yard and it looks as though it's in motion, as though there's a creature embedded in the rock. Today, somebody picked up the rock and looked at it, and inside a little cavern there were three little plants growing. Might that be one of the new plants?

In this particular case, the rock is supporting life because of dust, seeds and so on. Let's use this as an analogy. Where are they going to spring from? They will spring from unlikely places. The old plants, after all, had to tough it out in much harder times in the past when the Earth was less tolerant to life forms. So these plants will largely be coming up in the cracks in the sidewalks. They will be growing out of the cracks in the rocks. They will be growing in places that are so inhospitable that you cannot imagine that anything alive could grow there.

New Plants Will Be Extremely Hardy

Also, they will sometimes exhibit the most unusual features; that is, generally it is understood that if a plant's leaves are brown, it is dying. These plants will be able to grow to a stage where their leaves are brown but regenerate themselves. They will look like they are on the way toward falling, but they won't fall. They will be very hardy, very durable and initially misidentified as weeds. Of course, there are no such things as weeds; there are only plants that you don't know a use for or plants that support life forms that you may not recognize as being worthwhile.

What you're going to have here are plants that are so hardy they will grow in the snow. There will be ice all around them and you will look at those plants and you will not believe your eyes. These plants will grow in snow and ice and if a flood comes through and covers them up with water for three or four days, maybe three or four weeks, you'll say, "Well, that's the end of that plant." But when the water recedes, there it is, just like nothing ever happened. These plants are going to be highly durable. That's the important sign to watch for. They will have elements within them that will largely be edible (but by all means, have them checked first before you run out on the landscape eating everything in sight). They will have elements within them that will be able to stimulate that very therapy within you that will let you live without requiring as much water, without requiring as much food and certainly without requiring as much oxygen. In that sense, they are the end-time plants, the plants that mark the end of the need for oxygen dependence.

Remember, I said at the beginning, there's a safety net that's going to pull you up, help you to come up. On the next level of your existence, you're not going to have to deal with oxygen, so of course, you're going to live a lot longer. Oxygen is designed to support life in the forms you're in now, but also it's designed to limit life. Even in the best possible atmosphere combinations, with the body you have now, it's not going to allow you to live more than, at best, 150 years. It is a body that doesn't require oxygen at upper levels of your existence that you're working toward right now. You'll live a minimum 250 to 300 years. Of course you'll need the 250 to 300 years just to grow as much as you grow now, but that's another story.

Did I understand you to say earlier that the plant I asked about was not one of the new ones?

No, not one of the new ones, but it is illustrative of how these plants will grow that they will seem to grow in the most inhospitable of environments. That's most important. So, when you see plants, especially ones you don't recognize, growing out of places that you can't imagine could support life, such as a crack in the middle of the street, then give it a second look, especially you botanists out there.

Going back to gases and elements that are being released; in future times, how will they affect the human body?

Good question. These gases and elements that are coming up out of Earth to regenerate her will have initial effects. If you happen to be present when there is an earthquake or an Earth fissure and it is not a serious problem for life and limb, initially you might feel very short of breath, so back away from the fissure for a 24-hour period, because Earth will have to clear the passage. If you were to blow into a straw, in order to get the air from your lungs to come out of the end of the straw, you'd have to clear what's in the straw first. So initially what comes up from a fissure won't be easily breathable, but after that passage is somewhat cleared, there might be amazing regenerative effects.

In some cases, it might be colored water, very odd colors, unusual. You'll see odd light emanating from it, fluorescence. In other cases, it will be a definite odor, something you can smell. In still other cases, there will seem to be a substance near the surface. If you've never seen that substance before, don't touch it. If it's a smell, smell it. If it smells good, stay with it. But don't crowd around the hole, because remember, Mother Earth is bringing it up to regenerate herself. So just take a little bit. Of course, the chances of anybody's rushing over to one of these fissures and wanting to lean in for a good whiff are not high. After all, it will certainly be dangerous.

There will be waters that will find their way to streams and will initially appear to be polluting the stream. There will be fears by some people that an unknown pollutant is coming up or something stuck there a long time ago is coming up. That won't be the case, but it could change the color of your streams for a while. It could change them to red or to green, or even in some rare cases, especially in the northern hemisphere of the Earth, to violet. A striking color; the light shimmers off it and there are reflections. See if you can catch one on your body. It will make you feel better, invigorate you, give you a new lease on life. It won't work if the water was pulled out and bottled. It will work only if it is actually in the rivers or streams and sunlight is bouncing off of it. In other words, it has to be performing its function. Remember, all of these things are living elements of Earth, or in the case of the sun, a living element of the body of a living being.

They will be, in almost all cases, highly beneficial. So if you can experience just a little bit of it, it will have curative powers.

Will this happen in our lifetimes?

Yes. Oh, yes, I'm not talking about some vague far-flung future. I'm talking about earthquakes that will happen within the next three years. Recently, this person I'm speaking through revealed a vision he had had about a year ago concerning an earthquake in southern California and other places. I say that is the result of changes that are likely throughout '93, '94, '95, maybe as late as '97. Maybe they won't be quite as strong, and that's good, because we'd rather have more frequent, less strong earthquakes. But when they happen, gases will be released. All earthquakes that happen now will release gases. If you can rush over there within 24 hours and find the fissure, you can get a sample; you might catch something that hasn't been seen on the surface ever before.

You're talking about bringing things out of the Earth. Ar-

chaeologists are doing a lot of digging right now. Are they coming up with anything that will cause diseases?

No, fortunately. At the sites of archaeological digs, the process of life has evolved. Even if people died of diseases 800 to 900 years ago, or even just 300 to 400 years ago, those germs are not likely to be effective. Of course, if one were to suddenly open a large tombsite and take a deep breath, which archaeologists know better than to do, it could be a problem. But I do not perceive this as a serious problem. No.

However, there will be some people who will be digging down inside old volcanoes or old caves (possibly once upon a time a volcanic vent, but now largely regarded as a cave) who will find some well-preserved, naturally mummified ancient bodies. Those you must be careful with. If you're going to open up that body, kindly do so in a laboratory, all right?

What will we be breathing if not oxygen? Does it have a name yet?

It will have elements not unlike what you breathe now. You have gases in the air now. It will have some elements that don't really have a name yet, but it will not be something that oxidizes. It will tend to include elements that preserve. Now, some of you may have done some research into that; there are gases that tend to preserve organic matter. There will be variations of gases like that.

Formaldehyde?

No, no, no. Formaldehyde is not something that will be too comfortable for you to breathe at any time.

I've had two nights when I seemed to be unable to sleep, as if I were hyper, but I hadn't had any drugs or anything else that would cause that type of feeling. I was trying to get to sleep when all of a sudden there was a tremendous vibration, not up and down but horizontally, through the whole of my body. It was so strong that I thought it was an earthquake. It felt like my whole bed was shaking. I got up and saw nothing that would indicate that, turned on the radio to listen for reports and there were none. Then it happened again and my whole body just shook. I wonder if you think this is part of the changes or some other phenomenon?

This is not part of the changes of Earth, but I will comment on it because it is not an uncommon event right now. Long ago, a man channeled on this subject. He is passed over now, but I will discuss it.

Your universe, that which you know to be your matter, flexes and breathes not unlike all things flex and breathe with the pulse of life. You are going through an experience of moving from dimension to dimension. Of course you do this when you are asleep, but you are now going through this experience in a sentient way, you are alive, you are in your bodies, you are actually experiencing it, and not just as an out-of-body experience. You are actually experiencing a flexing of universal tension, and the universe is flexing faster now; it's like a pulse moving faster now than your universe normally moves. Your universe normally moves very slowly, as if you were breathing slowly.

To continue to use the breath example, it's as if you're doing this right now [pant, pant, pant] just that fast. When that happens, the universe has to reset itself. This normally happens between lives, but it's happening during life right now. So the reset mechanism is not unlike a medical practitioner's using an electrical current to stimulate the heart back into its normal beat. The universe is moving very fast, it's pumping itself up. And then zap, that feeling you feel physically, preceded by the tension. Zap. And then it begins to slow down. Maybe one zap does it, maybe it takes two. The universe slows down and resumes its normal rhythm, which is the intention of the electrical stimulation of the heart that a physician might use. That's what's going on here.

Why doesn't everyone feel it?

Because it is only felt by people who are rhythmically in tune with that at a given moment. The body's pulse and rhythm change. At any given moment within people's lives, they will experience this or not, depending upon their age, their physical condition, and their propensity to achieve an extremely relaxed state (sometimes called meditation). Some people do this before they go to sleep, but there's a wide range of factors. It does not have anything to do with how spiritual you are. It is almost as if the frequency — though it is not a frequency — is being played by your body at the same time and so you act as a tuning fork and resonate to that chord.

I'm wondering about New Zealand during the Earth changes.

New Zealand is a relatively safe place away from the things that everybody is exposed to, such as atmospheric changes, the ozone layer and all of that. New Zealand just happens to be located in a place where there is the birth of new life, but in this case, I do not feel that volcanic activities represent a great threat. However, the main thing that might be noticed is that 60 miles offshore to the east of New Zealand, there may be increased volcanic activity. I do not see it as a tidal wave threat, nor do I see it as an earthquake threat. It might simply be noticed on the scientific instruments. New Zealand is probably one of the safer places to be, from what I understand.

On the one hand I want to know about all the predictions and on the other hand, I don't.

This is a very important point. How much can you know that will help you, versus bringing about a mass-generated drama? We have one advantage working for us here: you are cycling through a time now when memory is changing its function. So we can talk about this and even if you work real hard at it, within five years you're not going to remember much of what was said, making books considerably more practical these days, I suppose.

Memory function itself is changing due to the fact that you are changing your entire thought structure and coming into what could be termed cubic wisdom, meaning the ability to use past, present and future combined with the total true mental consciousness of yourself. You are no longer required in a visualization-physicalization experience to make the dramas. So I would say that it is not at this time a serious threat, but it certainly would have been in the past. You are accelerating so fast, moving through potential and probable existences so fast, that you're really moving faster than your memory has the capacity to retain. So do not feel it's a serious problem.

By the way, have you wondered why my arm is up like this? In my time, I'm actually holding my pipe.

Isn't being psychic a touchy, tricky business?

It is very important that you believe only what feels good and comfortable to you. If something does not feel good and comfortable to you, if you do not have a corresponding gut feeling or heart feeling that something is true, or could be true, or is stimulating, may be worth thinking about, don't believe it. So my words to you are very simply this: If you do not have a good feeling about anything that is said here tonight, anything that is ever said in this fashion or anything that is ever said by a friend or anybody whom you now know or will know in the future, do not believe it and do not take it to be your own.

How can you know whether something is true or possibly interesting? If it is interesting you will think about it, and that does not create changes. Thought from the analytical level does not create changes. Change requires emotion. Only the feminine can create. Thought is masculine. It cannot create. I do not support the idea that thought creates reality, though I indulged the question because it was an interesting point. But I will not argue with you.

A lot of psychics are talking about earthquakes in California and a lot of people are afraid. I'm not buying into anything that everybody's saying anymore. I think it all begins with the self. And isn't there a point where Mother Earth and the spirit world get a little bit tired of the control element of our government? Aren't we responsible, too, and isn't there a bottom line where Mother Earth says, "This isn't going to go on anymore"?

Yes, but that "bottom line" has happened many times. When you go back in your written history, how far back can you really go? Not too far. That's because it's happened many times. Mother Earth has said, "That's enough of that," and leveled everything. But now you need, and Mother Earth recognizes that you need, to be able to go beyond chastisement from external sources. The baby that is scolded for sticking his or her finger into places where it doesn't belong eventually goes beyond that point and no longer requires an external chastisement and does not continue to stick fingers into the electrical outlet.

So it is time for mankind, the soul of the human being, to move beyond external force and to experience every single change as slowly possible so that you can change it in midstream. In a sense Mother Earth could have "popped off" long ago, leveled the place. That's easy for her, really easy. But because you are moving between dimensions, and because third-dimensional Earth is not actually your home right now, you are in a sense within the middle of that explosion. What happens in an explosion? You can take a film of an actual demonstration explosion and slow it way down. You can slow it down so far that you can actually experience all of the forces that lead up to the explosion, the explosion itself, the transformation of mass within the explosion and the resultant new material that exists as a result of the explosion.

So in a sense, you are in the explosion right now. You are in a loop of time in which that explosion is actually taking place. This loop of time has been created for you so that you have the opportunity as sentient beings to change the explosion itself, even though this loop of time will uncreate itself when you land at its point of termination which will be slightly before where you started that loop of time in the first place so that all the destruction that has taken place will not actually have taken place. You will learn your lessons. So the reason external chastisement is not taking place right now is so that you can move beyond childhood and be able to embrace harmony. That's why.

And thank you for bringing up the point about earthquakes. Remember, as has been stated by many people before, the whole purpose of the book of "The Revelation" is to encourage you to recreate the outcome. The whole purpose of catastrophic predictions, in the larger sense, is to encourage you to recreate the outcome. Don't buy into the catastrophe, as the publisher has stated many times in the editorial section of the *Sedona Journal of Emergence*; choose to recreate the potential.

I stopped work so that I could be of service. What more could I do to help us all evolve to a higher state?

Are there any other bodyworkers here? Any other therapists, any people in service? What can everybody do now? The main thing you can do when you are working with a client or a patient is to get into your balance. Don't synchronize yourself with the patient's imbalance. I recognize that in healers, bodyworkers, therapists, physicians, everyone. At best, you attempt to align yourself with the patient's best interest, or the patient's best health. But now the thing to do, because you will need your own energy, is to take five minutes between patients. Physicians sometimes might consider that a luxury, but certainly therapists and bodyworkers, give yourself time between the people you're working on. Replenish your body. Eat. Drink. Do your meditation before the people come. Come into your own best energy and do the exercise that we talked about. Call for the best beauty from your past, your future, the sun, the moon. Pull all of this into your body so that you can have not only your own balance, but more strength than you need. Remember, when you pull in that greater beauty, you'll only be able to use so much of it. The rest will radiate out into Mother Earth's body and for anything and anyone that is present, as well.

How can you know if this works? Certainly don't try it out on the guinea pigs of your patients. Try it out on your dogs, on your cats. Do the exercise when they're around. If you don't have a dog or a cat, go out into nature. Notice how the birds suddenly become happier, chirping louder, or becoming more quiet, very relaxed, mesmerized. Notice the effects on other life. Then try it with your clients. There will be a point at which you will be able to simply pull in the beauty of the past, pull in the beauty of the future, pull in the beauty and the strength of the sun, the renewal of the moon. It will be so natural. You'll be able to do it all the time. You will feel the warmth in your chest, the warmth in your solar plexus. The regeneration will love the spirit. It will do you good. The best any healer, bodyworker, physician can do right now is to do the best for yourself so that you have more strength than you need, so that strength, like heat and love, will naturally emanate from you every time you exhale. In that way, simply being in your presence will assist your clients.

Good night.

Recommended Reading

Hieronimus, Robert. *America's Secret Destiny.* Rochester, VT: Inner Traditions, 1989.

Jungclaus, David. *The Lemurian-Atlantean Vision Wheel.* Westlake Village, CA: Lost World Publishing, 1990.

Milicevic, Barbara. *Your Spiritual Child.* Marina del Rey, CA: DeVorss, 1984.

Roberts, Jane. *The Nature of Personal Reality.* Collegeville, PA: P-H Enterprises, 1976.

Shapiro, Robert and Rapkin, Julie. *Awakening to the Animal Kingdom.* San Rafael, CA: Cassandra Press, 1989.

Shapiro, Robert and Rapkin, Julie. *Awakening to the Plant Kingdom.* San Rafael, CA: Cassandra Press, 1991.

Shapiro, Robert. *The Explorer Race, Manual for Human Evolution.* Sedona, AZ: Light Technology Publishing, to be published.

14

Crystals

Dorothy Roeder

Crystals have fascinated people since the beginnings of life on Earth. Their beauty and durability have often given them great value. But we want to talk about their spiritual value, not their monetary value. In order to recognize the nature of their spiritual value we must first recognize that they, as well as everything else on Earth and in the universe, have life, or consciousness.

Crystals Have Souls and Consciousness

The consciousness of a crystal is not as fully developed as that of a person. It must be different, of course, because a crystal cannot see, feel or hear as we do, nor can it express itself as we do. It can only express itself at the physical level through its beauty and form. But at the soul level, it is a different story. At this nonphysical level of consciousness there is wisdom, knowledge and even will. This will is expressed as a desire to be physical and to reflect the beauty of the Creator and the Divine Plan.

Yes, contrary to what some may believe about life on Earth, there is a purpose to it which only the Creator can see perfectly. One purpose of life is to learn to understand who that Creator is, but it is so vast and has so many variations that billions of lives are needed to achieve this understanding. No individual consciousness can do it alone. Each must learn to tap into universal consciousness, offering his/her learning and wisdom before he/she can share that of the whole. Life may be experienced in humanoid form or as an animal, plant or mineral. Anything that has its own specific form can be thought of as reflecting some sort of guiding influence over its own existence and of having consciousness and the capability of evolving.

A crystal grows much more slowly than a person and is formed in a womb consisting of Earth itself: soil, rock, water. Somehow, the proper elements come together and precipitate out of their watery carrier, forming a wonderful array of beautiful and fascinating forms. Each place on Earth creates its own unique varieties, just as human parents create unique individuals in their own image. It is really more difficult to imagine how this could happen with such regularity by chance than it is to assume intention. Each place produces individual specimens that can be traced to their origins, but there are certain similarities that place them within the whole pattern of Earth's creations. Quartz has a basic six-sided crystalline form wherever it is found, but variations in that form make Arkansas quartz different from that of Madagascar or Brazil.

The consciousness that guides the building of form is soul or spirit. It is a higher consciousness that has awareness of subtle energies and dimensions beyond what we see at the physical level. This higher consciousness can see and understand the Divine Plan more completely than we can. Earth is a collection of many consciousnesses that have chosen to come together to work out the meaning and purpose of the Divine Plan. These many consciousnesses are divided into groups, sub-groups, sub-sub-groups and so on. The smaller working units are groups of individual consciousnesses associated with a particular place on the physical Earth. Each of these small groups maintains a connection to that higher level of consciousness which is more aware of the whole picture of what is happening on Earth. For humanity that is a group of divine beings called the Planetary Hierarachy, the White Brotherhood or perhaps the Brotherhood of Saints (Planetary Hierarchy might be best because it is certainly not limited to males). For crystals, the higher connection is an angelic being who serves as the consciousness of everything on Earth with a crystalline form.

This angel includes in its sphere of influence other angels who serve to guide specific kinds of crystals and, in turn, guide still others who make the sub-groups down to the place-specific groups. Those crystals that are developed enough in their form have their own angel who is part of the crystal hierarchy. So quartz has its own angel who guides all quartz crystals. There are many angels who work within its guidance as the guide for each specific place. For instance, unique quartz crystals are found near Herkimer, New York. Each one forms individually in its own "womb of clay." They are quite sparkly and are called Herkimer diamonds. As a group they are special, but in addition, each individual crystal is unique and has its own angelic consciousness. This makes them quite fun and useful to work with because they are able to focus on individual purposes. Quartzite, on the other hand, is a massive conglomeration of tiny crystals formed into one large deposit that could extend for miles. If you break off two pieces of a mountain made of quartzite, they would probably not have individual angels but would remain under the guidance of the angel of the mountain.

When a crystal forms on a substrate which connects it to many other crystals, it shares the consciousness of the whole group. If it should be broken off from the group it probably will develop a consciousness of its own and gain its own angel. When this occurs naturally underground, the crystal remains in the Earth and the broken area heals over, eventually forming another point on the broken end if there is time for it to continue growing. These crystals have time to become very secure in their own individuality; or you could say their individuality is very well expressed in their physical form. They are especially useful for healing because they have had the opportunity to learn to be perfectly whole in their individuality. A crystal that is dynamited out of the Earth and its substrate, on the other hand, may need to receive healing rather than be able to give it.

A crystal can be cut and enhanced by someone who tries to understand it so that it is not damaged but is given new life through the love of the person working with it. So the individuality of a precious diamond is aided in its development by a consciousness who has abilities it does not. Its power is refined and focused as it is carefully and thoughtfully cut by someone who understands it. The best gem-cutters may not recognize that they have been guided by the angelic consciousness of the crystal as well as their own knowledge and artistic sense, but they have learned to tune in at an intuitive level. Their love of their work allows them to help the gem perfect its understanding of itself and that is, ultimately, the goal of any consciousness. On the other hand a crystal that is badly cut may be unable to express truth as it sees it and this distortion of its energy makes it very difficult to use. It may bring "bad luck" to those who work with it, rather than protection and love.

How Do Crystals "Work"?

To understand how crystals can help us, we need to look some more at what consciousness is. Let's say for now that the perfect understanding of the Creator is Its consciousness and that is expressed through love. This love is greater than anything we can understand and must support the purposes of everything that is experiencing life, or consciousness. It becomes Light when consciousness directs it into a specific purpose. Then Light becomes the substance from which the universe and everything in it is made. Each one of us is Light and is created because of the desire of the Creator to expand its use of love. The Creator is always maintaining everything with a love that flows throughout everything that It has created. This love is present everywhere as a connection into the whole. It is an infinite, everlasting continuum that puts everything into contact with everything else.

Humanity, when it became physical, forgot that it was part of the whole, but crystals did not. Their physical bodies do not cut them off from the spiritual knowledge that they are still in the flow of universal love. They are a doorway into the wisdom and experience of the whole. You can connect into the flow of universal love without a crystal, but if you sometimes feel separated or even alienated from everything but your present experiencing, they can help you to feel reconnected. They do this by showing your subconscious, which runs your life and your body, how to connect with that universal flow at the physical and emotional levels. When you hold a crystal to seek help, to communicate or to admire its form, you make a connection with it that is formed from love. Your subconscious focuses in on the crystal and sees how it is flowing with its universal connection; then it realizes that it can do the same thing.

If you work with the crystal intently and consistently enough it will show you how to heal your own separation from the whole. It can help you to resolve your negative emotions into expressions of love. It can help you understand the meaning of who you are. It can help you restore the divine Light connection into your physical body so that your body can move out of the patterns of separation from perfection and begin to reflect the ideal. It can show you the crystal form of your own ideal and show you how to use it at the physical level.

To summarize, creation begins with consciousness. Thought and knowledge are aspects of consciousness. The basic stuff of which the universe is made is love because the Creator is love. That love becomes Light when it is transformed into objective purpose by will. Thought organizes this Light which comprises creation into shapes which are, to us, crystalline. Crystals therefore mirror the shape of the Creator's thought and reflect the shape of creation. Quartz represents the ideal expression of love at the physical level on Earth.

What Do Crystals Do?

We have talked mostly about quartz so far, because it carries the basic pattern of the ideal for humanity and Earth. The shape of the Light flow through its crystal matrix is so similar to that of your DNA that it moves and reflects Light in the same way. It doesn't distort the Light flow with hate, fear, loneliness and so forth, as you may be doing, so it can use the patterns of life the Creator has given it in the ideal way. Quartz, then, shows your subconscious, and therefore your body, how to use the ideal to create perfection in your body and in your life. It literally shows you how to flow the ideal at all levels of self and makes that ideal available to you. This subconscious recognition of how to use the ideal at levels that may not have seen it before will support other work you do to understand life and your divine purpose.

Other types of crystals complement quartz in showing you how to use Light. Calcite is almost as common as quartz and is a basic prototype for organizing the flow of Light. It shows your body how to use the electrical components of Light, while quartz manifests the basic fact that Light is electrical in nature. Calcite is important now because the Earth is moving into a new format of higher energy. You see it as moving into an area of space that is more radioactive. This is part of Earth's evolution in learning to use Light creatively, a sort of infusion of new material to keep things from getting stagnant. (You can't learn anything new if you just do the same things over and over, so the Creator keeps urging you along in expanding your potential by gradually giving you new things to work with.)

Calcite will help the body deal with the stresses of the new energies.

Green calcite is especially healing; pink shades help you deal emotionally with changes in your reality; yellow and orange calcites help your
mind to stretch its understanding of what is going on; brown and red
ones help you use the ability of Earth to ground electrical flow. All
kinds of calcite can do all these things, but the specific colors help
with special problems. White or clear calcite is the strongest organ-
izer of the electrical flow.

To return to quartz for a bit: it, too, is found in all colors of the
rainbow. Amethyst is a favorite of many and is another crystal that is
especially useful now in using the new energies. It shows you how to
clear out old energies and old patterns of thought and emotion that
are no longer needed. It emphasizes the new patterns being sent by
Light to heal, enlighten and guide Earth into its coming new form and
consciousness. Citrine promotes mental clarity and aids regeneration
and healing. These, with clear quartz, are the main varieties that form
prismatic crystals. Other kinds, such as rose quartz, can form crystal
shapes, but that is rare.

Rose quartz is usually found in shapeless masses. It is widely used
to open and heal the heart and show you how to be more loving. Most
other varieties of quartz fall into the chalcedony classification. They
are microcrystalline masses of very tiny crystals compacted together.
Actually, each of these tiny crystals has its own angel or consciousness,
but they are embryonic at this point and cared for by the greater angel
who ensouls the whole mass. When they are broken into smaller
pieces and shaped into pebbles by nature or carved by man, they can
begin the process of realizing their individuality and expanding their
consciousness. If you have one that you use and enjoy, you are
helping this process. Just as a child's perception of itself is enhanced
by its parents' love, so a stone learns what it is by sharing its Light with
you.

Some others of these microcrystalline varieties are jasper (red,
brown or yellow), chrysoprase (green), onyx (black or grey and white),
bloodstone (green jasper with red specks), carnelian (red-orange) and
agate (usually shades of grey, but also can include green or violet).
Onyx and agate are often dyed to make the common pieces more
interesting, but don't refuse to work with them for that reason. It
won't necessarily ruin them to make them more beautiful. See how
the stone feels to you and let that be your guide, rather than someone

else's beliefs. The dye is only on the outside, after all. They are all healing, energizing, balancing and uplifting. They are complete in their ability to recognize the whole ideal, but each has special uses for which it is particularly adapted.

Selenite is another mineral that is very useful now. It is also called gypsum and is used to make plaster, cement, pottery and fertilizer, so it is all around you in altered states. It comes in some very interesting crystal forms also and is most impressive when fixed in a stand so light can shine through it. Selenite can help you transcend the barriers of your present set of limitations and move through the varying frequencies and dimensions of expanded awareness. It helps you to accept that you are a multidimensional being and that your physical body is only part of what you really are.

Space is limited here so all the crystals that can be useful for you cannot be discussed, but there is one that has a special place in humanity's present evolution. That is tourmaline. It is valuable in balancing the male and female polarities, the receptive and dynamic principles of Light. Tourmaline helps to integrate your own polarities and make you feel more balanced. It helps you to establish a more secure base of creativity within yourself so you can think and act more effectively. It comes in several colors — black, green, pink and blue. The watermelon variety includes green and pink and is especially good for integrating all aspects of self. The blue has a very spiritual energy and can help bring love into your life in very practical ways. Black tourmaline serves as a sort of "air cleaner," soaking up negative vibrations and transforming them into positive ones.

How to Choose a Crystal

You are the best one to choose your own crystal. It is sort of like choosing a mate. Others may think they know best, and maybe they do, but you won't ever be really satisfied unless you choose them yourself. If you are the sort of person who prefers to let others make your decisions, crystals can help you learn to rely on your own feelings and knowledge. We would suggest that quartz is a good first choice because its uses are so basic, but if you feel drawn to something else, go with that.

If you find your own crystal in the Earth and dig it yourself, you become the crystal's mother in a sense, because you have brought it out of its womb. Such a crystal is special and can "bond" with you so that it understands you and your problems in a very personal way. Carving or shaping a stone for yourself can produce similar results if the stone agrees to the process. How do you know what a stone wants? Listen to it by paying attention to your feelings about it. Don't let your desires override other messages that may be coming to you.

Accepting that a crystal does have consciousness and its own purpose or will is probably the first step in choosing the right one for yourself. By recognizing that its needs are as important as your own, you can form a working partnership that will help you both. Crystals, remember, are using love unconditionally, so they will usually do whatever they can to help you achieve your purpose. If you are choosing to align with the Divine Plan, it will be easy to work with them because they are flowing the Light of that plan as their consciousness and form.

If you don't have the opportunity to go out and dig for crystals, you may receive one as a gift or you may buy one. Let your intuition be your guide here. Often, you might look at what is available and immediately pick up one and hold it. Then you will start looking for the right one. Your mind starts working on finding what is "right" and seeks out the advice of someone who is supposed to know which one is best. You must realize that you already know and are holding it.

Quartz that has "clouds" in it and is not completely transparent will tend to hold energy and a program better. Clear ones are the best transmitters. The huge "Earthkeeper" quartz crystals are not clear and are already programmed with vast amounts of knowledge about Earth's past, present and future. They work by keying into specific aspects of the knowledge of the whole, the Akashic Records, and transmitting that information to those who are ready for it. As you work with crystals, you will find that many have specific programs they are working on, but they will be willing to fit yours into what they are doing. You will find the right one because your soul and that of the crystal will work together to help you find each other.

Cleansing Your Crystal

Once you have found your crystal you need to make it part of your self. If you dug it yourself, washing off the dirt will be sufficient cleansing. As you carry it in your pocket or hold it, you become acquainted and get used to each other. That is all that is necessary. If you bought it, it may need to be cleaned. There are various ways to do this. Primarily, you want to get rid of any energy that may be sticking to it that is not compatible with your own. One good way is just to hold the crystal in your right hand and imagine Light flowing from you into the crystal, sweeping away anything that is not needed. You can also hold the crystal under running water while doing this. Salt water has traditionally been recommended, but it should be very dilute and is not often necessary. Too much salt distorts the crystal's energy. If you need soap or solvent to clean it, that's okay; follow with water and Light.

Some crystals like time in the sun periodically to realign with its light. This is very energizing for clear quartz, but will cause amethyst to fade. (Don't heat your amethyst either or it will lose its color.) Other crystals like moonlight. If a crystal has been abused or misused it might benefit from being buried in the Earth for a time — three days to a few weeks. Again, let your intuition be your guide. If you need energy from the Earth, burying your crystal for a time may help it bring you that energy. But crystals are already quite comfortable with being physical; after all, they've been in the Earth for thousands, maybe millions of years already. They accept that they are part of Earth, and all crystals are already "grounded." The burying process is usually more for you than for the crystal.

Not much "sticks" to transparent crystals. They are clear transmitters. Dark or opaque ones may need to be cleaned periodically with Light or water. If you have some sort of polarizing device, that would be very useful also. You can make your own polarizer by getting some copper wire and making it into a loop that is big enough to pass the crystal through; or just move it over the crystal a few times. This will realign the crystal's energy without damaging any patterns you may have set up for working with it. Black obsidian is a good stone for removing negativity, but it tends to hold on to energy. If you let sit for a time the negativity will dissipate, but if you use it intensely, it needs to be cleansed often and the copper coil is one good way to do that.

Using Crystals

The most important thing to do when using a crystal is to let it know what you want to do with it. If you want it to help you heal yourself or someone else, tell it so. If you want it to help you communicate with friends or teachers in other dimensions or levels of spiritual reality, it can do that if you ask it to. If you want it to help you focus your meditations, let it know. Choose your crystal with its purpose in mind, if possible. Some crystals can do many things, but most will be more effective if you do one thing at a time and give yourself and the crystal some time to work out the best relationship.

You need to be clear in your own mind about what you want to do. The crystal can help you do that. If you want it to do something that is inappropriate or impossible, it will let you know. It can't do any thing for you. It is not magic in itself. The magic happens when you are able to use your full creative potential to achieve what you want or need. The crystal can help you learn to do that or help you connect with someone else who can.

Don't be too specific about exactly how you want to accomplish what you and the crystal are planning, unless you are very experienced or have specific guidance from an expert. Once you have decided on what you want to do, let the method of doing it evolve on its own. You might use a technique you learned from someone else as a starting point, but don't be rigid in its use. If variations begin to occur to you, try them and see how they feel. What works best for someone else will not necessarily be best for you. Do try to observe with all your senses, even your unconscious ones, how the process is working. The more you are open to the flow of the process at all levels, the more you will learn about what is going on at all levels. Practice plus being open to new ways of looking at things will create the vision and the wisdom you seek.

In meditating with a crystal, many find it helpful to hold one or to hold one in each hand. If you are learning to channel, crystals can help you feel secure about connecting with an energy that seems to be outside yourself. They can't make any connections for you but they can show you how they connect with the creative flow of consciousness that is always available everywhere. Imagine the Light from a divine source flowing into your crystal, lighting it up and making it radiant. Then imagine your whole self responding to that flow in the same way. You can also set the crystal in front of you with a light behind it or under it to make the image more real. If you practice meditation with your crystal regularly, I guarantee you something positive will happen. It won't be the same for everyone and it may not be clearly definable. Again, don't expect any particular set of events beyond your defined purpose or you may set up limits on what you can achieve.

Crystals for Healing

We have already mentioned that self-healed crystals are good for healing. Madagascar quartz works very well. Boji stones are very good at taking away pain and balancing energies. They don't need to be charged; just let them know what you want by placing them over the area that needs to be healed. A small crystal can be charged for healing. Hold it in your dominant hand and imagine love and healing Light flowing from the universe through your heart and into the crystal. When you feel that you are finished, place the crystal wherever healing is needed, either on yourself or on another.

You don't have to be in contact with another to heal him or her. You will need some sort of request or agreement from him or he will not be open to receiving the healing. When you are ready, simply charge the crystal with healing Light as before and imagine placing the crystal wherever it is needed. You can also imagine the person standing in front of you and send the Light through the crystal to him. If you don't have his permission, send the energy to his soul and ask it to use the energy in an appropriate way. Never use a crystal to try to force on someone else something he does not want. If what you want is not part of that person's consciousness or will, it will not work and his energy structure will not accept it. Crystals focus energy very specifically and will intensify any negative repercussions that come back to you. However, if your intentions are loving you will not have to worry about harming anyone. You do have to allow another to use the energy you send in whatever way he finds best, even if that is not what you desire. As you practice with crystals, the gifts of knowing and seeing how they work will come.

When using crystals for others, be sensitive to their feelings. Crystals have been used as weapons in the past, and if someone who has been injured by one believes you are harming him, it is possible that you will do so. You need to be clear in your motives also. Many of us have subconscious problems that can influence our better, clearer intentions. If something should go wrong, look very carefully inside yourself to see where the problem might be. As you bring more Light into yourself by working with crystals, problems will come up that you must accept and, eventually, release. This is good and a benefit of working with crystal energy, but may not always be comfortable. Let the crystals help you clear confusion and negativity out of your Light field.

There are many books with good information about using crystals for almost any purpose. Some of them are listed at the end of this chapter. We are able to give only a few basic ideas here to try to get you started.

Crystal Elixirs

Crystal elixirs should be mentioned. Basically, they are water that has been charged with the energy of specific crystals. Water is almost magical in its ability to accept and hold different energies and transfer them wherever needed. You can simply set a glass of water in the sun with the crystal in it for a few hours. Then drink it or rub it over an area that needs it. In Atlantis, bottles or bowls were often carved for the purpose of making elixirs, but you don't really need anything that elaborate.

Amethyst would be a good one to start with. Its elixir will help cleanse your cells of impurities and release negativity while bringing in new, higher energy. Peridot elixir is also very good for healing and energizing your cells and balancing their energy flow. It helps the DNA align with the ideal in Light and release imperfect patterns of using Light. Moonstone makes an elixir that is especially good for calming emotions and bringing in a more balanced perspective. Clear quartz will help clear and balance your drinking water in general. It is a good idea to keep one in your water jug.

Crystal Grids

Quartz is usually the foundation of any crystal grid pattern. Its hexagonal shape mirrors the basic shape of the Divine Plan which flows as Light, so three-, six- and twelve-sided grids are the easiest to work with. Three crystals set equidistant from each other will help you manifest a particular purpose or thing. Six would form a six-sided star, the symbol of balance, so would be good for healing the mind and calming emotions (Figure 1). Twelve make a more powerful grid that connects into the divine archetypes at a higher, more comprehensive level, but that may bring more of your divine potential into your life than you are ready for, so work with the simpler patterns first. A circle of twelve is excellent for groups though, because there are more people to handle the expanded potential. Each person's weak areas are supported by the strengths of another.

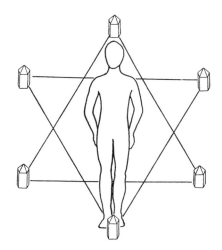

Figure 1

Four quartz crystals make a square configuration that fits into the flow of the plan at the physical level. It

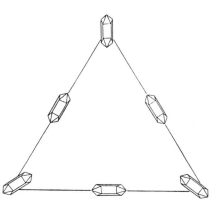

Figure 2

brings out your power as a part of the Earth. It interacts at a physical level but is difficult to combine with spiritual purpose. You will need an interdimensional approach to do that — thus the pyramid, square base with triangles on all sides. If you suspend a crystal over the center of your square crystal grid you can bring a more illuminated viewpoint to your work at this physical level (Figure 2).

The pyramid is the first step to truly interdimensional awareness: thus the current fascination with them. As humanity seeks to expand its awareness and knowledge into new dimensions, the pyramid is the

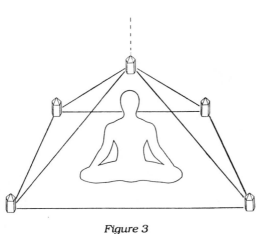

Figure 3

key. If your crystal pyramid grid is large enough, it is good to meditate in. Quartz carved into pyramid shapes or crystals that form pyramids naturally, such as fluorite or apophyllite, can be worn. They create a multidimensional energy field that helps you work at levels of expanded consciousness.

If you are a beginner, choose crystals that are similar in size and shape. Use doubly terminated ones for healing grids or generators (crystals that stand upright) for a pyramid base, for instance. As you learn to be sensitive to the specific energy of each crystal and how they are interacting, you can get more creative with your grids. You can introduce other minerals than quartz into them to add to their healing, balancing or inspirational qualities. You can increase the number of quartz crystals without changing the basic quality of the grid energy if you don't change the basic geometric shape (Figure 3).

Crystal Cocreators

Crystals are not magic and will not do anything for you. They are wonderful tools that can assist you in doing your best to realize your full divine potential. They will help you to express your abilities to the extent to which you are willing to go with them. They can be mirrors that teach you that you are Light and show you the ideal you hold within yourself. They can become good friends and coworkers you feel comfortable and familiar with as you take more responsibility for making the world a better place. They can be a key to knowledge that the world needs now at this critical time of great changes. They can be a connection with Earth that helps you to be a more effective cocreator with her.

If Earth is going to reach the full potential of these new times, we all, as part of Earth, must do our share. Crystals are part of the consciousness of Earth, along with humanity, plants and animals, and we must learn to work consciously together with Earth to create a place where all can be free to realize their full creative potentials. Humanity, as the most evolved part of Earth's consciousness on the physical level, bears the most responsibility for preserving and assisting its evolution. The crystal kingdom is willing to do its part to help us and is very eager to share love in as many ways as is possible here.

Admiring and using crystals is one way of acquiring knowledge from many dimensions, past, present and future, that will help us to promote that evolution.

Recommended Reading

Alper, Frank. *Exploring Atlantis.* 3 vols. Phoenix, AZ: Adamis Int'l., 1990. History of the use of crystals in Atlantis; crystal grids and healing.

Baer, Randall N. and Vicki V. *Windows of Light.* Out of print. But see the *Crystal Connection: A Guidebook for Personal and Planetary Ascension.* San Francisco: Harper, 1987.

Bailey, Alice. *Esoteric Healing.* New York: Lucis Publishing Co., 1953. Channeled from the Tibetan Master Djwhal Kuhl. All of Alice Bailey's books are an important part of the basic structure of New Age spiritual thought and systems. This one is a little easier to read than others.

Gerber, Richard. *Vibrational Medicine.* Santa Fe, NM: Bear & Company, 1988. A scientific review of alternative healing methods, including crystal techniques and New Age healing techniques.

Gurudas. *Gem Elixirs and Vibrational Healings,* Vols. I and II. Boulder, CO: Cassandra Press, 1985. Information channeled by Kevin Ryerson.

Lyman, Kennie, ed. *Simon & Schuster's Guide to Gems and Precious Stones.* New York: Simon & Schuster, 1986. The physical properties and descriptions of virtually every crystal you might ever see. The best part is that each entry is illustrated by a color photo.

Mondadori, ed. *Simon & Schuster's Guide to Rocks and Minerals.* New York: Simon & Schuster, 1978. The physical properties and descriptions of virtually every crystal you might ever see. The best part is that each entry is illustrated by a color photo.

Plummer, Gordon L. *Mathematics of the Cosmic Mind*. Wheaton, IL: The Theosophical Publishing House, 1970. The mathematical symbolism of Blavatsky's Secret Doctrine is translated into the geometric shapes of the universe and its energy essence.

Sheldrake, Rupert. *A New Science of Life*. Los Angeles: Jeremy P. Tarcher, Inc., 1988. Distributed by St. Martin's Press, New York. Sheldrake's theory of "morphogenetic fields" describes how the form of a whole group is shaped by the thought, activity or evolution of its parts.

Wood, Elizabeth. *Crystals and Light*. New York: Dover Publications, Inc. 1977.

15

Life Behind Sleep

Marlene Myhre

It's a funny thing about humankind — most of us still insist that the time we spend on Planet Earth is reality! However, one by one, young and old, we are awakening to a voice of truth within that is guiding each of us through a search for higher understanding. These awakenings may be through a near-death experience, the appearance of a holy or angelic spiritual figure in a vision or meditation, or step-by-step daily feedback from behind sleep — that which most of us would call the dream. I consider the dream to be the clearest access to the Creator's direction and also the fastest way to rid the individual soul of its fears and habits while it resides on Planet Earth.

I was handed an invitation to join a group of people who meditated every day at 7:00 a.m.

Many dreams similar to the one above are quite clear in their overall message. Others, as in the example below, are so precise in their specific guidance for the dreamer's spiritual development that it takes an experienced esoteric dreamworker to translate the images in their entirety.

The townspeople had gathered at the restaurant for breakfast before going on to work. They were seated outside. I had my purple nightgown on. As I walked through the group before going inside, I noticed I then had on white two-piece pajamas.

This is the time that St. Paul referred to as the "outpouring of the Spirit," meaning this is the time that the Creator's gifts of enlightenment are accessible to the masses of humankind. The New Age is not a particular kind of person, idea or school of thought, but a time when the whole of humanity matures as souls. It is a time of being open, honest and individually responsible with our talents, our knowledge and our life's circumstances. Our efforts are acknowledged and further guided through the direction received from behind sleep.

I was at home showing the house to a group of people. There was a small chapel upstairs with the bedrooms. As the people inquired about space to stay, I told them there were no extra rooms except for the chapel upstairs.

A brief translation of this dream tells us that the dreamer is consciously recognizing the presence of her intuitive aspects and her ability to use them. She is putting the whole of her mind to sacred use and all parts of her being are in agreement. As a result, I would counsel her with methods to exercise her intuitive impulses so that she actively uses her inner knowing.

The perpetuation of the belief that only the physical, material part of our existence is reality is the most grievous error currently holding us in mental bondage today. Those of us who insist on disbelieving anything that cannot be seen, heard or felt with the physical senses deny the primary premise and promise of God, that "I am with you always." We thereby forgo the joyful truth that the Creator can and will commune with us and will forever retain contact with us in our dense forms by way of prayer, meditation and dreaming.

In brief, when each of us, as a soul, descends into the shell of a baby's body at birth, we are contracting for a few years' experience in the denseness of life, the densest and most solid of God's creations, to see if we then can remember our roots, our Source, and to see if we can remember to use the tools provided this physical form to initiate contact with that Source whenever it is needed.

How do we rediscover all that is out there as we awaken the urge to explore through our now dense physical form? And how do we avail ourselves of the answers to our prayerful requests, concerns and contemplations? We must go into the mind, yes, but not through the mental processes that most of us use daily. We must use the intellect only to push through our self-imposed boundaries into Consciousness (with a capital C), into a space of receptivity. For those who feel that is too much work or takes too much time, the oversoul still provides feedback to our every thought, question and musing through the dream.

This grand New Age is the time we have all been praying for, and awareness of it is seeping gradually into the slowly awakening consciousnesses of a very materialistic humanity. We have prayed for wisdom, foresight, courage, understanding and peace for ourselves and our world. And yet, when given direction personally in the funny, current, insightful, attention-getting ways of the internally residing spirit, many of us still insist we "do not dream." Others of us who do remember our dreams will psychoanalyze individual symbols or ignore the gift entirely until it just fades away, waiting for a time of better receptivity. It may sneak through the walls of consciousness later as an "idea," but then without the detail or vividness given earlier.

I was sleeping when a man broke into the house. I could hear him in the kitchen looking through my refrigerator and wondered if he would find me here.

This is a classic picture of a latent talent trying to be recognized and put into action in this dreamer's life. This dreamer stays hidden and avoids confronting new opportunity which would certainly result in spiritual growth. Often I can see the issue intuitively and will aid the dreamer to begin seeing for herself

The Most Personalized Gift of the Holy Spirit

The dream is the most personalized gift of the Holy Spirit available to us, yet rather than study and attempt to understand it more clearly, many of us still turn our backs on the richest resource of spiritual understanding we have.

How much easier could it be? Our souls speak to us in our own language by forming the thought of the Creator into a picture-story personally meaningful to each dreamer! It is just like having a handheld language computer when traveling to a foreign country, but better. The dream takes the voice of God, the Creator of our being, and translates that voice into not just English, French or Portuguese, but also into pictures, into local dialects, or into our own personalized "slanguage," if you like. The precision of our dream guidance is amazing.

I am the first to acknowledge the difficulty most of us have in psychoanalyzing dreams. Consider, however, that that method was just a first step in Western culture's validation of the dream. Freud and Jung introduced to this culture the idea of a Universal Intelligence from which we as humanity draw our inspiration. The dream was honored as a very important voice of that Intelligence. However, we proceeded to use human concepts to understand and translate the concepts of God, or Universal Intelligence. The reading of the dream esoterically, when it has been recorded immediately upon awakening, clearly describes the human form as including a physical, emotional, mental and soul body, all as operative forms within the physical body and each with ever-changing polarities.

Fears of the Past

The recurring dreams of the child are usually pictorial reviews of particular fears held from past embodiments of that soul that must be removed and replaced with trust in the Plan of the Creator. We have felt so separated from our Creator over the eons that many of us have lost our knowing that as souls we are eternal creations. That feeling of separation colors our every thought and our every reaction to life's trials. We try to believe, through a variety of religious dogmas and creeds, that we will return to the Creator, but that belief is so weak that the consummate fear of humankind at this stage of our development is fear of annihilation of who we are. We fear the shedding of our physical body because we think we are the physical body. We have forgotten that we are an eternal soul that rises up and out on the last day of physical embodiment. The mistranslations of current scriptures have left those whose inner voice is undeveloped in much darkness.

I was in church attending my father's funeral (he had died two years earlier). All of a sudden my father sat up, got out of the casket and walked as though in full health (This scene has been recurring every few months since his death.)

This is a dream confirming that Helen, as we'll call this dreamer, still viewed her father as dead (buildings indicate state of consciousness). The pictorial message to Helen shows that her father is very much alive, even though his form as she knew it is no longer physically present to her. She is being shown as graphically as possible that she should "see" him as alive.

It is interesting to note that as soon as I translated this dream, which Helen accepted with full understanding, the recurring dream no longer appeared. Her soul was then free to go on to other teachings and understandings.

Many of the dreams we fear the most, simply from ignorance, are repeatedly showing us our ongoing and eternal life. We call prior experiences past lives, but in truth we have only one life. We live a continuous existence in which we, as creations put forth by God, continually expand. explore, seek, search, understand and grow in loving wisdom as a result of our experiences. Until mankind understands this basic truth, we will continue to see dreams and visions of "the dead" rising, waking and walking.

The dream is the pictorial summarization used by the soul to ignite and retain our interest in our higher mind. Unfortunately, most of us have a well-bred capability of tuning it out. There are many spiritual and religious people among us, but most are still spiritually ungrounded as we view "life" out of very human eyes.

Inventions, Discoveries and Creativity

I was mixing xxx, yyy and zzz and knew this would be a wonderful and healthy fast-food snack for children. Someone said I should distribute it through Bashas' (an Arizona food chain). They would be interested.

How many of us would act on a dream like this? All great technological advances, without exception, become implanted into our brains first by the activities of the higher mind behind sleep. We do not have to be "religious" to tap into Universal Intelligence, but we are required to use any knowledge, once given, with brotherly love and responsibility.

Many great men and women among us have been given insight into solving human problems through contemplative insights and dream inspirations. However, many of the most humanitarian and thus spiritualized human beings have lived earthly lives of great courage, as required by the sharing of new teachings. Often, they also lived under dehumanizing circumstances of ridicule, scorn or political judgment for their efforts to awaken humankind. Gandhi, Schweitzer, Einstein, Tesla, St. Francis of Assisi, John the Baptist, the Wright brothers and Martin Luther King are just a few. We are given personal guidance, inventive insights and philosophical training, yet we seldom honor those who honor their own inner voices.

Beliefs keep a population in line and regulated, but beliefs also create fears and misconceptions. Unless we search within ourselves for truth, we remain intellectually disconnected from our Creator. Beliefs create a full house in that place known as purgatory when our individualized soul does not recognize its responsibility to actively plan its own participation in the heaven-worlds of our continual life.

My dear friend Susan was getting ready to pass over. She told me she was ready but would miss me. We decided we wouldn't let distance interfere.

If we truly experienced an ongoing communicative relationship with Source, we would no longer grieve departing loved ones. If we truly understood continuing, eternal life, we would not beat ourselves with the belief of unworthiness. Nor would we put off until tomorrow the joy we could be experiencing today, in this part of eternity. Most of us consider that eternity starts sometime in the future! Let us contemplate that for a moment. Isn't reality a happy thought?

Realizing Heaven's Consciousness

The dream time is an entrance into just the beginning of a continuing mind link with the Universal Intelligence.

I often think that most of us feel that we're "down here" someplace without our headsets on. The truth of the matter is that the human body and its consciousness is a perfect receptor for the love and the energy and the understanding of God. It's just that most of us do not yet know it, having discarded most of our rich dream lives. We have been told to live by our consciences, yet in many ways we invalidate that conscience, particularly when we say it was "just" a dream.

It is not a gift to remember where we go as souls or with whom we commune behind sleep. It is a natural function of the soul. It requires little effort. We are taught that God answers prayers. But do we listen for those answers? There are many ways for our Creator to speak to his creation, but we have come to believe that we are not worthy of His/Her time and attention; and assuming He/She could not be bothered with our little lives, we also take little time to listen.

The details of advice given in dream surpass those given by any source outside of ourselves. Until each of us accepts our own divine nature and honors our own internal mechanisms for retrieval of information, nothing that any one else can give us by way of advice can impact us as much as our own soul guidance.

The pictorial is, of course, subject to as much mistranslation as the human mind can choose to conjure up. It also has the richest feedback. Truly, each picture is worth at least a thousand words of universal wonderment.

We must begin. We can begin by keeping our own dream journal. My translative methods are a most definitive process; however, there are many good teachers available. While we are compiling a record of our own dreams, even without a teacher, we can ask for understanding and translations to be revealed within the dream itself. We can begin simply by being curious about where we go and what we do behind sleep!

I wish you wonderful adventures.

Recommended Reading

Chaney, Earlyne. *Initiation in the Great Pyramid.* Upland, CA.: Astara, 1987.

A Commentary on the Book of the Revelation. Virginia Beach, VA: A.R.E. Press, 1945.

Evans-Wentz, W. Y., ed. *The Tibetan Book of the Dead.* London: Oxford University Press, 1960.

The Holy Bible, King James Version. New York: American Bible Society.

Lamsa, George M. *Gospel Light.* San Francisco: Harper SF, 1986.

The New American Bible. New York: Catholic Book Pub. Co., 1970.

Papastavro, Tellis. *Gnosis and the Law.* Tucson, AZ: Balkow Printing Co., 1972.

Prophet, Elizabeth Clare. *The Chela and the Path.* Los Angeles: Summit University Press, 1975.

Sechrist, Elsie. *Dreams, Your Magic Mirror.* Chicago: Contemporary Books, 1990.

Spangler, David. *Revelation: The Birth of a New Age.* Elgin, IL: The Lorian Press, 1976.

The White Brotherhood. Washington, DC.: Millennium Publishing House, Inc., 1975.

16

Rebirthing

Alice Tickner

Rebirthing is a type of therapy that helps us to discover the inner being. It allows us to get in touch with beliefs and memories we are holding in our subconscious minds. The feelings based on these beliefs are literally trapped into the cells of our bodies.

Rebirthing involves two people — a rebirther and a client. You, the client, lie down on a bed or couch and are allowed to feel cozy by being covered with a blanket. At this point the rebirther will probably connect physically with you, holding your shoulder or arm, for example, and then surrounding the two of you with white Light for protection. This is a good time to call upon any guides or masters whose presence you would like and to give thanks for any answers or guidance you receive during the rebirthing session.

The two of you may or may not have discussed beforehand any specific answers you are looking for. When I started rebirthing as a client, I sometimes had a specific question. Other times I was willing just to let the process unfold. Either way is fine.

Changing Your Future by Examining Your Past

The rebirther may wish to continue physically connecting with you or not. Again, whatever the two of you are comfortable with is fine. You now begin to be guided by the rebirther into connected breathing. Each client and each rebirther is different and each session will be different from the others. Sometimes, as a rebirther, I talk a lot during the session: other times I talk very little. Some times you will breathe for only a short time (five or ten minutes) before you're ready to delve into your mind or before emotions start welling up to the surface. Other times you will need to be taking in the breath for twenty to twenty-five minutes before your mind calms down from everyday chatter and you are ready to get in touch with something from your past that you need to resolve. There will be times when you will be guided to breathe into your solar plexus and other times when you will be guided to breathe into your heart center. A good rebirther will be psychically connected to you and will know when to guide you to breathe slower or faster. Each session is unique and it will flow in whatever way it is meant to.

When you are ready, you might be guided back to a past experience or to some part of the brain or belief system that needs to be illuminated with Light and love. I usually guide my clients to visualize descending a staircase while I count backwards from twenty to one. When I get to one I snap my fingers, and the client is usually envisioning and/or feeling some past experience that has not been resolved or to which there is some great emotional attachment. (The rebirther must always be aware when doing this process that you, the client, can sometimes go back into a past life. It is important to understand this because if you are experiencing, for example, sexual molestation in a past life by someone you are close to in this life, confusion could arise.) Going back to that situation might cause emotions such as sorrow, fear, guilt or anger to spring to the surface. What is important is that those emotions be allowed to be really felt and thereby released. The rebirther can provide you with a pillow you can scream into (since most of us do not have the luxury of rebirthing in a place where we can scream our heads off without the noise affecting other people). If you start crying, tissues are available to wipe away the tears, and if you feel guilt or fear, the rebirther supports you in feeling those emotions.

What is most important is that the void created by the releasing of those feelings be replaced with love, joy and forgiveness. This, too, is accomplished through breathing guidance by the rebirther. It can be aided by visualization or a guided meditation. I can remember one session as a client when my whole body filled up with God's love. It started at my feet and flowed all the way to the top of my head. In fact, not every breathing session will bring up negative emotions — not that any emotions are negative, as they are all part of the God in us, but let's face it, some are harder to feel than others. I have experienced sessions in which the whole hour was about recharging with God's love. There is nothing like the natural high obtained through the breath!

A session may provide you with mental discoveries about yourself. It is only through the self-discovery process that you can know and therefore love who you are. Once you have done that, you can give yourself permission to change any part of your thinking and behavior. Any change that brings more joy and happiness into your life is what rebirthing is all about.

Let me give you one example of a self-discovery I made during the breathing process. I remembered that one Christmas when I was about three years old, which would have made my two older sisters eight and thirteen, I received a little red wagon. My parents were really broke and my two sisters received very little by comparison. I paid so dearly for that little red wagon because of the reactions of my two sisters, that I made a choice never again to have more than they had (or more than anyone else had, for that matter). Having more made me feel unsafe. This one simple realization unlocked many keys to self-understanding. Discovering the complicated web of beliefs in my mind and the emotions I had locked inside made the rebirthing process invaluable.

People have often asked if rebirthing is comparable to hypnotism. I would have to say that although there are similarities, rebirthing is much, much more. In rebirthing, you have greater control because you are using a special breathing technique that allows you to become involved. This technique is called "integrated breathing" or "connected breathing" and is something that can not be explained on paper but must be experienced. Do not ask how "the breath" works because it is one of those unexplainable gifts. Nor will I attempt to convince you, because it would be like trying to convince you that such a thing as God exists.

Those of you who have difficulties doing the integrated breathing usually have a difficult time surrendering to the love that is available to you; consequently your resistance to healing is also greater. If you can inhale and exhale the breath of life at a deep level, the results are also deep.

If you decide to try rebirthing on your own, you probably are a person who believes you have to do everything on your own and do not deserve to be supported by another person, much less by God. So my recommendation is that even though you may think that you can do it on your own, don't. Take advantage of all the love and support you can receive from a good rebirther.

Rebirthing is not for the meek and mild. It is often a traumatic process that will put a lot of upheaval into your life. There may be avalanches and rock piles left to clean up, but it can move mountains. However, don't expect those mountains to move during the course of one or two sessions. It takes lifetimes to weave the web of the subconscious mind, and it is certainly going to take more than a couple of sessions to untangle that web, understand yourself and release all emotions unrelated to love. (I rebirthed for a year and a half.)

At this point you might be saying to yourself, "Well, if it's that traumatic, why should I bother?" My answer is simple: It is the quickest, most effective way I have ever experienced to get to know yourself. Unless you know yourself and what that intricate mind of yours believes, how in the world can you expect to know what to do to change your life?

You Create Your Own Reality

I personally will take a rebirthing client only if she or he understands that she/he creates her/his own reality, one hundred percent. Not ninety-nine point five percent, but one hundred percent! If you are driving along the highway and a car comes around the corner on your side of the road and crashes into you, on some level you have agreed to have that happen in your life. If you don't understand that, then how can you expect to understand that you have total control of what happens in your life? You need to accept totally the concept that there is no such thing as an accident before you can know that you are God.

If at this point you have a desire to rush off and scream into a pillow that you think that I'm a complete jerk or at least totally crazy, then by all means rush off and do it. Then please come back and read the previous paragraph again because *it is really important that you understand that you create your own reality one hundred percent.*

You will never know that you have the power within you to be, do or have, whatever you want until you grasp this concept. And once you do grasp this concept then you will know that you have the power to change your life.

Once you know that you have the power and are willing to take total responsibility for your life, you will also know that if you don't like what you have been creating in your life, you can change it. Change yourself through love on the inside and you will see the world outside of you reflect those changes.

Be Kind to Yourself

While you are waking up and discovering that you do create your own reality is not the time to get into self-blame. Oftentimes you don't want to accept that you've created your own reality because you don't want to take responsibility for the mess that you've created in the past. No! No! No! That is not what this is all about. This is the time to rejoice in your freedom and to know that the future does not have to reflect the past. The only moment you have is now so don't regret the past. By taking responsibility, you can look forward to the journey, knowing that you can forgive and release anything you don't want and make room for all the love you want now and in the future.

Knowing you create your own reality clarifies, does it not, why rebirthing is so effective? It allows you to discover the beliefs, angers, fears, shames and sorrows that have created that reality. Then you can release them and change your life.

You Must be Willing to Change Your Life

Now let's talk about the importance of willingness. Unless you are willing to heal your life, you can try every trick in the book and your mind will not create any healing. And how do you tell if you are willing to heal your life? Start by being totally honest with yourself. How much effort are you willing to put into the healing process?

A few years ago I was totally broke and had no mode of transportation, but I hitchhiked over fifty miles into the city and paid fifty dollars a session because I was very willing to change my life. So if something comes up that gets in the way of your rebirthing session or if it looks like lack of money is the issue (which it rarely is) then take a second look at how willing you are to heal your life. Rebirthing is a very healing process but it is one that demands that you tell yourself the truth. Start now by telling yourself the truth about how willing you are to heal your life.

What will happen if you go through discovering what an awful being you are? If you're loving yourself at a high level you will do just that...go through it. You see, if you knew you were God, or perfect unlimited love, you probably wouldn't even be in your body. At the best you would be pure white Light, but at the very least you'd be happy, healthy, abundant, in wonderful relationships and knowing exactly why you are here on this planet. Therefore, it is going to be just fine if you see what you think is the awful, unloving you, because you will know that it is only one of the layers covering up the real truth about yourself: You are perfect unlimited love.

As the process of rebirthing unlocks your subconscious mind, it is a good idea to understand that your mind is like an iceberg. One-seventh of it is like the part you see above water, your conscious mind. The other six-sevenths are like the rest of the iceberg beneath the surface — your subconscious mind. Now picture a scale with one-seventh of your mind on the conscious side and six-sevenths on the subconscious side. Be patient with yourself because it will take a long time for the scale to tip. Remember that you have been carrying these ideas around in your subconscious for all of your life, maybe many lifetimes. Even when you think you have discovered most of what has been lurking beneath the surface, you will find that it takes time to integrate these ideas into your life. Patience is important at this time.

It is also important that you have a very good rebirther to work with. He or she will be there to love and support you and remind you that you are a wonderful human being, especially at those times when you don't feel very wonderful at all.

Another thing to be aware of during the self-discovery process of rebirthing is that even when you think you have changed your mind about something, whammo! The old idea can come back and smack you right in the face. Staying with the earlier example, let's say you have discovered that you have carried a strong belief all your life that said you shouldn't have more than people around you. You have been working hard on changing that belief and understanding that there is an abundance for all of us. You've even gone out and bought a new car. You know you deserve it and you are totally enjoying it when the old mind-set kicks in: "You shouldn't have more than your brother." The next thing you know you have created having your brand new car creamed by a snowplow while the car is parked in front of your house. Do not despair. If you persist, you will eventually change your mind to the point where it embodies the change so completely, even you won't be able to get in the way of yourself.

Choosing a Rebirther

How should you choose your rebirther? If it is important to you that someone have a degree, then by all means go for that, because you probably will not allow it to work with someone who does not have that qualification. My priority would be to work with someone who has experienced rebirthing and has used it to better her/his own life. I always suggest that potential clients have one session with me and see how they feel. I also think it's important that a rebirther love doing the work. That love allows a level of unconditional love with which she or he can support you in discovering your true self.

If, after one session of rebirthing, you and the rebirther trust each other and are comfortable with each other, I suggest that you make a commitment to do a series of sessions, preferably once a week. I find that somewhere between the third and the sixth session, fear will rear its ugly head. Unless you have made a commitment to do a series of sessions, it will be easy to quit. Quitting is an individual choice, of course, but if you don't keep going, you'll never make it through to the other side of the fear.

If you find the rebirther teaching that he or she is your source of love instead of supporting you in the knowledge that you are your own source of love, take a quick hike, for your own sake. You have all your own answers and a rebirther should be there to support you in discovering them. This does not always mean telling you what you want to hear. It does mean telling you the truth, even if it is not necessarily what you want to hear.

If you have a session with a rebirther and she or he doesn't feel right for you, then go find someone else. Just remember that everyone is a mirror and you have put that person in your life in order to learn a lesson.

Feel It and Deal With It

Even though we know that we create our own realities, it is important that we allow ourselves to feel any anger and blame that arise. This is not the time to let your head get in the way and tell you that since it was your creation, you should not blame anyone else. That is the truth, but blame and anger can be literally stored in your cells, and you need to feel them in order to release them at a deep and real level. If you flip into your head at that point, the necessary releasing will not occur. If you are encountering negative feelings toward people from your past, it is best if you can stay away from them until you have worked through to the other side. It is difficult for people when you are dragging up garbage from your past about them. But remember, this is your journey, not theirs. If you keep going you will get to the other side where you are taking responsibility at a deep level for your part in your experiences. More often than not, after you have worked through to the positive side of those experiences, you will be able to let love flow with that person, as well as others, in a way you have never allowed it to flow before. What a gift that is!

Rebirthing is one of the greatest gifts you can give yourself, a way to support yourself at one of the highest possible levels. Rebirthing is a quick and effective way of understanding the inner you. Although learning to love yourself is a continuous journey, rebirthing can be a giant step along the way. If I have encouraged you to experience rebirthing, I am thankful. It is your life and only you can change it. Good creating!

Recommended Reading

Orr, Leonard and Ray, Sondra. *Rebirthing in the New Age*. California: Celestial Arts, 1978.

17

Creative Visualization

by Glenn Phillips

Creative visualization is the technique of visualizing what you wish to have in your life and then mentally and physically turning that wish into reality.

You are already using this power. Everybody daydreams in one form or another; it is called the power of imagination, and it is the creative power of the universe. We all have it and we all use it. Creative visualization is simply using this power in a conscious and positive manner and taking control of our own destinies.

Unfortunately, most of us have deep-seated feelings of inadequacy. We don't feel we deserve to have more in our lives, to be prettier, to have more meaningful relationships, or to have vibrant good health. All of these things are possible. The universe is bountiful. Everything you could wish for is available to you, you simply have to really want it and be totally willing to accept the best the universe has to offer.

All creative activity starts as a thought: "I think I'll make a cup of tea" precedes actually putting the kettle on to boil. "I would like to go somewhere warm" precedes going out and buying a ticket to Hawaii or starting to save up for the trip. Creative visualization is taking a particular thought and turning the energy of that thought into reality. Often when we think of visualization we think in terms of career goals, winning the man or woman of our dreams and, of course, the biggie, riches. All of these things are possible, but so are many, many more. Your life can be changed in a multitude of ways.

Creative Visualization and Health

You can create your own good health. Unfortunately, the reverse is also true. All too often we create our own ill health. To prove to yourself the power the mind has over the body, there is a simple exercise you can do. For a whole day, try telling yourself how tired you are. Feel the tiredness throughout your whole body: "Man, am I ever tired. I'm absolutely exhausted. I'm so tired my joints ache. Boy, will I ever be glad when this day is over." Keep repeating this and you'll find yourself dragging your tired, aching body into bed by the end of the day. Now try the reverse for a day. Tell yourself how great you feel. Stand in front of your mirror and praise yourself. Feel your energy level climb. Note the difference.

Further proof of the power your mind holds over your body is the fact that when testing new drugs, doctors disregard any success rate lower than twenty percent. They have found that twenty percent is the normal success rate when administering placebos. Disease is really just "dis-ease," and if you can get rid of the reason for the dis-ease the disease will often follow suit. There have been many documented cases of "incurable" illnesses being cured with the aid of positive creative visualization. Space does not allow me to list them here but the authors recommended at the end of this chapter list many such instances.

Creative Positive Visualizations

In order to use this power, to harness it, you must first learn to relax deeply. Relax deeply and imagine that which you wish to bring about. Then picture that wish in the most vivid detail you can.

There are many ways of relaxing deeply and the one I most often use is included at the end of this chapter, but if you have one of your own, then by all means use the one that works best for you.

The subconscious, that part of your brain you are "reprogramming," cannot tell the difference between fact and fantasy, so in effect what you are doing here is changing your "fantasy" into "fact."

When stating your dreams or your goals, use positive words; for example, "I am now creating a better life for myself," rather than, "I am now going to leave my old shabby life behind." It is believed that the subconscious mind does not register negative words. Thus, it is not useful and might even be detrimental to form an affirmation such as "I am not afraid." The subconscious hears "I am afraid," so instead it must be turned around so that it becomes "I am filled with courage."

You should also remember always to visualize in the present tense, or to put it another way, always see your dream as a positive established fact; for example, "I am now creating a better life," or "My life is wonderful, I now have a great life," rather than "I am going to have a better life" or "Someday I will have a better life." It is very easy to get caught up in systematic thinking. Often when we want something good to happen for us, we automatically think of it as happening in the future; but if we visualize it in this manner it will very likely stay in the future.

Decide what you wish to create, but try to be realistic in your goals and focus your energy on one thing that you would like to have happen. Avoid splintering your energy. For example, if you were to say to yourself, "I will improve my relationship with my spouse, I will get that promotion at the office, and I will improve my golf game by four strokes," it would water your energy down to where none of these things would be likely to happen. You can, of course, make them all happen, but work on them one at a time.

Write down your goal on a piece of paper. Be precise and try to form this visualization in one simple sentence. It is very helpful at this point to take the sentence, or at least the key words, and post it in a place or in several places where you will see it often. This helps reinforce your visualization, and it always pays to jog your subconscious as often as possible.

Start out by creating easy goals. One that I have found that you can have a lot of fun with is car-parking spaces. Needless to say, I wouldn't recommend meditating while driving, but as you approach the mall, create a parking space close to the front entrance. See the vacant space waiting for you as you drive up; see a car pulling out just as you arrive; see yourself pulling into the empty slot. If it doesn't happen every time, don't get down on yourself and don't give up. Make a game of it. Have fun with it and you'll soon be amazed at how often it works.

A Word of Warning

Remember always that creative visualization cannot be used to the detriment of any other person; in fact just the opposite is true. If you have someone in your life with whom you are not getting along, whether it be in a personal relationship or in a work environment, if you send negative thoughts toward that person those negative thoughts will come back to you, whereas if you send out thoughts of love, those thoughts will come back to you tenfold and in ways that you might not even imagine.

Your ability to create is infinitely more powerful than you have allowed yourself to realize. Use this power always for good and your efforts will be answered with a fuller, more rewarding future.

Creative Visualization and the Lottery

Just another word of caution here: creative visualization will not necessarily help you win the next lottery. Let me explain. What we think we want, especially on the superficial level where, unfortunately, we spend most of our time, and what we think we need to make us completely happy may not be what truly will bring us the greatest satisfaction or even the greatest happiness.

We all accepted — no, requested — this lifetime to work on our own personal growth, as well as to work out karma from previous lifetimes. If what we are visualizing is not in harmony with those plans we set for ourselves then it is not likely to happen. However, if we truly believe, and I am now talking again about that part of us that is deep inside and always true to our best interests, that winning a large amount of money will help our growth and our journey toward discovery, then we just might win that big jackpot!

Visualization by Itself Is Not Enough

It would be nice if we could simply visualize what we would like to have occur and then just sit back and wait for it to happen but, like most things in life, it doesn't work quite that way. Abigail van Buren once said, "If you want a place in the sun, you have to put up with a few blisters." First we have to visualize it and then we have to help it happen, but while we are helping it happen we must continue to "see it, feel it and be it."

Sometimes we know what we want but are unable to see any way of bringing that dream about. Don't let that stop you. Visualize it anyway. See it as an accomplished fact and continue to work on the visualization. It is sometimes true that the larger the objective, the longer we have to work toward its fulfillment. As long as your dream is real, logical and not against your life plan, work on it and it will come about.

When I say you have to help it along, what I mean is that if you're a twenty-five handicap golfer and wish to be a fifteen handicap, then don't take a month off to visualize it and then expect to go out and break eighty. Visualize it, see yourself accepting the club trophy if you will, but at the same time continue to practice.

Obviously, if you visualize the impossible — if you're a fifty-five year old woman and you visualize yourself winning the Miss Teenage America pageant, it isn't going to happen. Try instead for the Woman of the Year Award.

If it doesn't happen right away, don't give up. If a dream is worth having it is worth waiting for, and if your timing is not quite right, have patience with the universe. Remember that the universe has everything in it that you could ever need or desire; you only have to want it and be willing to accept it as it is given. Continue to visualize your goal regularly while you strive toward helping it to happen.

Here's a worthwhile exercise: write down your visualization on another piece of paper. Be specific, go into as much detail as possible. If you are trying to improve your lifestyle, spell out the ways in which you can see this happening. Now periodically re-read this visualization, this "daydream." One of the truly great things about creative visualization is that it allows us to see our own growth. It allows us to see how our route to our destination in life changes. So often, what we want today is not what we will want tomorrow. Our goal, whether or not we are truly aware of that goal, stays pretty much the same but our path toward it constantly changes.

The Technique

If possible, at least at first, choose a darkened room, and sit or lie in a comfortable position, making sure to keep your back as straight as possible, as this helps the flow of energy. If you find that you tend to fall asleep while lying down then try sitting upright. Relax and take a deep breath. Let it all the way out slowly and when you feel that it is all out, contract your stomach and chest muscles and push it even further out. Follow this with several more normal slow deep breaths; five or ten should suffice.

Allow your eyes to close slowly as you do this and feel yourself slowly unwinding, feel your body relaxing. You are now putting yourself into an altered state. Some would call this a state of meditation, others would call it self-hypnosis. It is, in fact, both. It is the relaxed state used by almost all metaphysical self-awareness practices, whether it be channeling the higher spirits, communing with your inner self, or even just relaxing to eliminate daily stress.

Once more, I would like to say that this is the particular self-relaxation method I use, but if you have one that works for you, then by all means use that one. If possible, I would recommend making your own tape and playing it during this process. If you happen to find that one of the excellent tapes available commercially suits your requirements, then use it. The advantage of a tape is that it is repetitious and that it allows you to relax without having to remember your lines.

Start to relax your body by beginning at your feet and working your way upward. Say the words to yourself, either out loud or silently, whichever feels better: "I feel my feet relaxing...totally relaxing. I feel the relaxing power working its way up my legs. My lower legs are now totally relaxed and my upper legs are now starting to relax." Get the picture? Work your way up through the whole body, ending with the facial muscles. It is surprising how we can think we are totally relaxed and then find that we are still sitting with our mouth or jaw rigid. You can now see the advantage of having this on tape.

At this point I prefer to protect myself mentally. I mentioned earlier that we must not project negative thoughts, for to do so will prove harmful to ourselves. However, there are negative entities, just as there are friendly entities, and in this relaxed state we are more vulnerable to both.

I am not trying to alarm anyone, and as long as these steps are taken, it is perfectly safe. Also, if this protective practice is always part of our relaxing technique, it soon becomes second nature and helps the whole procedure.

What I do is to see myself completely surrounded by a bright white Light. I envision this white Light encompassing my whole body and

I say the following words to myself: "My body is now completely surrounded by a bright white Light. I can see the Light. It is surrounding my whole body and only my own spirits and those who wish me well can reach me through this protective white Light. I am calm, I am sure, I am open to the universe."

Continue to breath slowly, and with each exhalation feel yourself going inward (or downward, if you wish), feel yourself going into that spot at the very center of your being. As you enter that spot there are many paths to choose from. You may have chosen what you wish to visualize ahead of time and if that is the case then simply let your thoughts turn to this visualization. Remember to see it, feel it, be it.

Once you've practiced reaching this spot and find you can get there easily, you can also use this state to get answers that you can get no other way. Ask your question and wait. Don't get discouraged at this time if you don't get a clear mental picture or "visualization." The answer may come in words, it may come in pictures or, as is usual for me, it may simply come as an intuitive knowing. It may come and go so quickly that you may miss some or all of it, but it will come. If at first you are not satisfied with what you are receiving, keep practicing. Don't give up on the universe. Remember always, it is all there for you to have, you just have to truly want it, visualize it, and work toward it, and it will be yours.

Recommended Reading

Gawain, Shakti. *Creative Visualization.* New York: Bantam Books, 1978.

Siegel, Bernie S. *Peace Love and Healing.* New York: Harper and Row, 1989.

Bry, Adelaide. *Visualization – Directing the Movies of Your Mind.* New York: Harper Collins, 1979.

18

Beliefs Can Heal Your Life

Louise Hay

Life is Really Very Simple. What We Give Out, We Get Back

What we think about ourselves becomes the truth for us. I believe that everyone, myself included, is 100% responsi- ble for everything in our lives, the best and the worst. Every thought we think is creating our future. Each one of us creates our experiences by our thoughts and our feelings. The thoughts we think and the words we speak create our experiences.

We create the situations, and then we give our power away by blaming the other person for our frustration. No person, no place and no thing has any power over us, for we are the only thinkers in our mind. We create our experiences, our reality and everyone in it. When we create peace and harmony and balance in our minds, we will find it in our lives.

Which of these statements sounds like you?

"People are out to get me."

"Everyone is always helpful."

Each one of these beliefs will create quite different experiences. What we believe about ourselves and about life becomes true for us.

The Universe Totally Supports Us
in Every Thought We Choose to Think and Believe

Put another way, our subconscious mind accepts whatever we choose to believe. They both mean that what I believe about myself and about life becomes true for me. What you choose to think about yourself and about life becomes true for you. And we have unlimited choices about what we can think.

When we know this, then it makes sense to choose "Everyone is always helpful," rather than "People are out to get me."

The Universal Power Never Judges or Criticizes Us

It only accepts us at our own value. Then it reflects our beliefs in our lives. If I want to believe that life is lonely and that nobody loves me, then that is what I will find in my world. However, if I am willing to release that belief and to affirm for myself that "love is everywhere, and I am loving and lovable," and to hold on to that new affirmation and to repeat it often, then it will become true for me. Now loving people will come into my life, the people already in my life will become more loving to me, and I will find myself easily expressing love to others.

Most of Us Have Foolish Ideas About Who We Are and Many, Many Rigid Rules About How Life Should Be Lived

This is not to condemn us, for each of us is doing the very best we can at this very moment. If we knew better, if we had more understanding and awareness, then we would do it differently. Please don't put yourself down for being where you are. The very fact that you have found this book and have discovered me means that you are ready to make a new positive change in your life. Acknowledge yourself for this. "Men don't cry!" "Women can't handle money!" What limiting ideas to live with.

When We Are Very Little, We learn How to Feel About Ourselves and About Life by the Reactions of the Adults Around Us

It is the way we learn what to think about ourselves and about our world.

Now, if you lived with people who were very unhappy or frightened, guilty or angry, then you learned a lot of negative things about yourself and about your world. "I never do anything right." "It's my fault." "If I get angry, I'm a bad person."

Beliefs like this create a frustrating life.

When We Grow Up, We Have a Tendency to Recreate the Emotional Environment of Our Early Home Life

This is not good or bad, right or wrong; it is just what we know

inside as "home." We also tend to recreate in our personal relationships the relationships we had with our mothers or with our fathers or
what they had between them. Think how often you have had a lover
or a boss who was "just like" your mother or father.

We also treat ourselves the way our parents treated us. We scold and
punish ourselves in the same way. You can almost hear the words
when you listen. We also love and encourage ourselves in the same
way, if we were loved and encouraged as children.

"You never do anything right." "It's all your fault." How often
have you said this to yourself?

"You are wonderful." "I love you." How often do you tell yourself
this?

However, I Would Not Blame Our Parents for This

We are all victims of victims, and they could not possibly have
taught us anything they did not know. If your mother did not know
how to love herself or your father did not know how to love himself
then it would be impossible for them to teach you to love yourself.
They were doing the best they could with what they had been taught
as children. If you want to understand your parents more, get them
to talk about their own childhoods; and if you listen with compassion,
you will learn where their fears and rigid patterns come from. Those
people who "did all that stuff to you" were just as frightened and
scared as you are.

I Believe that We Choose Our Parents

Each one of us decides to incarnate upon this planet at a particular
point in time and space. We have chosen to come here to learn a
particular lesson that will advance us upon our spiritual, evolutionary
pathway. We choose our sex, our color, our country, and then we look
around for the particular set of parents who will mirror the pattern we
are bringing in to work on in this lifetime. Then when we grow up,
we usually point our fingers accusingly at our parents and whimper,
"You did it to me." But really, we chose them because they were
perfect for what we wanted to work on overcoming.

We learn our belief systems as very little children, and then we
move through life creating experiences to match our beliefs. Look
back in your own life and notice how often you have gone through the

same experience. Well, I believe you created those experiences over and over because they mirrored something you believed about yourself. It doesn't really matter how long we have had a problem or how big it is or how life-threatening it is.

The Point of Power Is Always in the Present Moment

All the events you have experienced in your lifetime up to this moment have been created by the thoughts and beliefs you have held in the past. They were created by the thoughts and words you used yesterday, last week, last month, last year, 10, 20, 30, 40 or more years ago, depending on how old you are.

However, that is your past. It is over and done with. What is important in this moment is what you are choosing to think and believe and say right now. For these thoughts and words will create your future. Your point of power is in this present moment and is forming the experiences of tomorrow, next week, next month, next year and so on.

You might notice what thought you are thinking at this moment. Is it negative or positive? Do you want this thought to be creating your future? Just notice and be aware.

The Only Thing We Are Ever Dealing With Is a Thought, and a Thought Can Be Changed

No matter what the problem is, our experiences are just outer effects of inner thoughts. Even self-hatred is only hating a thought you have about yourself. You have a thought that says, "I'm a bad person." This thought produces a feeling, and you buy into the feeling. However, if you don't have the thought, you won't have the feeling. And thoughts can be changed. Change the thought, and the feeling must go.

This is only to show us where we get many of our beliefs. But let us not use this information as an excuse to stay stuck in our pain. The past has no power over us. It doesn't matter how long we have had a negative pattern. The point of power is in the present moment. What a wonderful thing to realize! We can begin to be free in this moment!

Believe It or Not, We Choose Our Thoughts

We may habitually think the same thought over and over so that it does not seem we are choosing the thought. But we did make the original choice. We can refuse to think certain thoughts. Look how often you have refused to think a positive thought about yourself. Well, you can also refuse to think a negative thought about yourself.

It seems to me that everyone on this planet whom I know or have worked with is suffering from self-hatred and guilt to one degree or another. The more self-hatred and guilt we have, the less our lives work. The less self-hatred and guilt we have, the better our lives work, on all levels.

The Innermost Belief for Everyone I Have Worked With Is Always, "I'm Not Good Enough!"

We often add to that, "And I don't do enough" or "I don't deserve." Does this sound like you? Are you often saying or implying or feeling that you are "not good enough?" But for whom? And according to whose standards?

If this belief is very strong in you, then how can you possibly have created a loving, joyous, prosperous, healthy life? Somehow your main subconscious belief would always be contradicting it. Somehow you would never quite get it together, for something would always be going wrong somewhere.

I Find that Resentment, Criticism, Guilt and Fear Cause More Problems than Anything Else

These four things cause the major problems in our bodies and in our lives. These feelings come from blaming others and not taking responsibility for our own experiences. You see, if we are all 100% responsible for everything in our lives, then there is no one to blame. Whatever is happening "out there" is only a mirror of our own inner thinking. I am not condoning other people's poor behavior, but it is our beliefs that attract people who will treat us that way.

If you find yourself saying, "Everyone always does such and such to me, criticizes me, is never there for me, uses me like a doormat, abuses me," then this is your pattern. There is some thought in you that attracts people who exhibit this behavior. When you no longer think that way, they will go elsewhere and do that to somebody else. You will no longer attract them.

Following are some results of patterns that manifest on the physical level: Resentment that is long held can eat away at the body and become the disease we call cancer. Criticism as a permanent habit can often lead to arthritis in the body. Guilt always looks for punishment, and punishment creates pain. (When a client comes to me with a lot of pain I know they are holding a lot of guilt.) Fear and the tension it produces can create things like baldness, ulcers and even sore feet.

I have found that forgiving and releasing resentment will dissolve even cancer. While this may sound simplistic, I have seen and experienced it working.

We Can Change Our Attitude Toward the Past

The past is over and done. We cannot change that now. Yet we can change our thoughts about the past. How foolish for us to punish ourselves in the present moment because someone hurt us in the long-ago past.

I often say to people who have deep resentment patterns, "Please begin to dissolve the resentment now, when it is relatively easy. Don't wait until you are under the threat of a surgeon's knife or on your death bed, when you may have to deal with panic, too."

When we are in a state of panic, it is very difficult to focus our minds on the healing work. We have to take time out to dissolve the fears first.

If we choose to believe we are helpless victims and that it's all hopeless, then the universe will support us in that belief, and we will just go down the drain. It is vital that we release these foolish, outmoded, negative ideas and beliefs that do not support us and nourish us. Even our concept of God needs to be one that is for us, not against us.

To Release the Past, We Must Be Willing to Forgive

We need to choose to release the past and forgive everyone, ourselves included. We may not know how to forgive, and we may not want to forgive; but the very fact that we say we are willing to forgive begins the healing process. It is imperative for our own healing that we release the past and forgive everyone.

"I forgive you for not being the way I wanted you to be. I forgive you and I set you free." This affirmation sets us free.

All Disease Comes from a State of Unforgiveness

Whenever we are ill, we need to search our hearts to see who it is we need to forgive. *A Course in Miracles* says that "All disease comes from a state of unforgiveness," and that "Whenever we are ill, we need to look around to see who it is that we need to forgive." I would add to that concept that the very person you find it hardest to forgive is the one you need to let go of the most. Forgiveness means giving up, letting go. It has nothing to do with condoning behavior. It's just letting the whole thing go. We do not have to know how to forgive. All we need to do is to be willing to forgive. The universe will take care of the hows.

We understand our own pain so well. How hard it is for most of us to understand that they, whoever they are we need most to forgive, were also in pain. We need to understand that they were doing the best they could with the understanding, awareness and knowledge they had at that time.

When people come to me with a problem, I don't care what it is — poor health, lack of money, unfulfilling relationships, or stifled creativity — there is only one thing I ever work on, and that is LOVING THE SELF. I find that when we really love and accept and APPROVE OF OURSELVES EXACTLY AS WE ARE, then everything in life works. It's as if little miracles are everywhere. Our health improves, we attract more money, our relationships become much more fulfilling and we begin to express ourselves in creatively fulfilling ways. All this seems to happen without our even trying.

Loving and approving of yourself, creating a space of safety, trusting, deserving and accepting will create organization in your mind, create more loving relationships in your life, attract a new job and a new and better place to live and even enable your body weight to normalize. People who love themselves and their bodies abuse neither themselves nor others. Self-approval and self-acceptance in the now are the main keys to positive changes in every area of our lives.

Loving the self, to me, begins with never, ever criticizing ourselves for anything. Criticism locks us into the very pattern we are trying to change. Understanding and being gentle with ourselves helps us to move out of it. Remember, you have been criticizing yourself for years, and it hasn't worked. Try approving of yourself and see what happens.

Holistic Healing Recommendations

Body

Nutrition: Diet, food combining, macrobiotic, natural herbs, vitamins, Bach Flower Remedies, homeopathy

Exercise: Yoga, trampoline, walking, dance, cycling, Tai Chi, martial arts, swimming sports and so on

Alternative Therapies: Acupuncture, acupressure, colon therapy, reflexology, radionics, chromotherapy

Massage and Bodywork: Alexander, Bioenergenics, *Touch for Health*, Feldenkrais, deep tissue work, Rolfing, polarity, Trager, Reiki

Relaxation Techniques: Systematic desensitization, deep breathing, biofeedback, sauna, water therapy (hot tub), slant board, music

Books:

Airola, Paavo. *How to Get Well.* Sherwood, OR: Health Plus, 1974.

Bieler, Henry G. *Food Is Your Best Medicine.* New York: Ballantine, 1987.

Hay, Louise. *Love Your Body.* Carson, CA: Hay House, 1989.

Royal, Penny C. *Herbally Yours.* Provo, UT: Sound Nutrition, 1982.

Simonton, Carl. *Getting Well Again.* New York: Bantam, 1982.

Mind

Training: Affirmations, mental imagery, guided imagery, meditation, loving the self

Psychological Techniques: Gestalt, hypnosis, NLP, Focusing, T.A., rebirthing, dream work, psychodrama, past-life regression, Jungian therapy, humanistic psychotherapies, astrology, art therapy

Groups: Insight, est, Loving Relationship Training, ARAS, Ken Keyes Groups, all 12-Step Programs, AIDS Project, rebirthing

Books:

Bry, Adelaide. *Visualization: Directing the Movies of Your Mind.* New York: Harper Collins, 1979.

Fankhauser, Jerry. *The Power of Affirmations.* J. Fankhauser, 1979.

Gawain, Shakti. *Creative Visualization.* New York: Bantam, 1978.

Gendlin, Eugene. *Focusing.* New York: Bantam, 1981.

Gillies, Jerry. *Moneylove.* New York: Warner Books, 1988.

Hay, Louise. *Heal Your Body.* Carson, CA: Hay House, 1988.

Jampolsky, Gerald. *Love is Letting Go of Fear.* Berkely, CA: Celestial Arts, 1988.

Jampolsky, Gerald. *Teach Only Love.* New York: Bantam, 1984.

Keyes, Ken. *The Power of Unconditional Love.* Coos Bay, OR: Love Line Books, 1990.

Price, John R., *Superbeings.* Boerne, TX: Quartus Books, 1981.

Ray, Sondra. *Celebration of Breath.* Berkely, CA: Celestial Arts, 1983.

Ray, Sondra. *Loving Relationships.* Berkely, CA: Celestial Arts, 1980.

Spirit

Prayer: Asking for what you want, forgiveness, receiving (allowing the presence of God to enter), accepting, surrendering

Spiritual Group Work: M.S.I.A., T.M., Siddah Foundation, Self-Realization Fellowship, Religious Science, Unity

Books:

A Course in Miracles. Glen Ellen, CA: Foundation for Inner Peace, 1975.

Addington, Jack and Cornelia. *Your Needs Met.* Marina del Rey, CA: DeVorss, 1982.

Any book by Emmett Fox

Holmes. *The Science of Mind: 50th Anniversary Edition.* New York: Putnam Pub. Group, 1989.

Roberts, Jane. *The Nature of Personal Reality.* Collegeville, PA: P-H Enterprises, 1976.

Yogananda, Paramahansa. *Autobiography of a Yogi.* Los Angeles: Self-Realization Fellowship, 1981.

Some Points of My Philosophy

I have long believed:
"Everything I need to know is revealed to me."
"Everything I need comes to me."
"All is well in my life."
There is no new knowledge. All is ancient and infinite. It is my joy and pleasure to gather together wisdom and knowledge for the benefit of those on the healing pathway. I dedicate this offering to all of you who have taught me what I know: to my many clients, to my friends in the field, to my teachers, and to the Divine Infinite Intelligence for channeling through me that which others need to hear.

We are each 100% responsible for all of our experiences.
Every thought we think is creating our future.
The point of power is always in the present moment.
Everyone suffers from self-hatred and guilt.
The bottom line for everyone is "I'm not good enough,"
It's only a thought, and a thought can be changed.
Resentment, criticism and guilt are the most damaging patterns.
Releasing resentment will dissolve even cancer.
When we really love ourselves, everything in our life works.
We must release the past and forgive everyone.
We must be willing to begin to learn to love ourselves.
Self-approval and self-acceptance in the now are the key
to positive changes.
We create every so-called "illness" in our body.

In the infinity of life where I am, all is perfect,
whole and complete,
and yet life is ever changing.
There is no beginning and no end,
only a constant cycling and recycling
of substance and experiences.
Life is never stuck or static or stale,
for each moment is ever new and fresh.
I am one with the very Power that created me and this Power
has given me the power to create my own circumstances.

I rejoice in the knowledge that I have the power
of my own mind to use in any way I choose.
Every moment of life is a new beginning point
as we move from the old. This moment is a new point
of beginning for me right here and right now.
All is well in my world.

In the infinity of life where I am,
all is perfect, whole and complete.
I believe in a Power far greater than I am that flows
through me every moment of every day.
I open myself to the wisdom within,
knowing that there is only One Intelligence
in this universe. Out of this One Intelligence
come all the answers, all the solutions,
all the healings, all the new creations.
I trust this Power and Intelligence,
knowing that whatever I need to know is revealed to me
and that whatever I need comes to me
in the right time, space and sequence.
All is well in my world.

In the infinity of life where I am,
all is perfect, whole and complete.
Each one of us, myself included, experiences the richness
and fullness of life in ways that are meaningful to us.
I now look at the past with love and choose
to learn from my old experiences.
There is no right or wrong, nor good or bad.
The past is over and done.
There is only the experience of the moment.
I love myself for bringing myself
through the past into this present moment.
I share what and who I am,
for I know we are all one in Spirit.
All is well in my world.

Deep at the center of my being there is an infinite well of love.
I now allow this love to flow to the surface. It fills my heart,
my body, my mind, my consciousness,
my very being and radiates out from me in all directions
and returns to me multiplied. The more love I use and give,
the more I have to give.
The supply is endless.
The use of love makes me feel good,
it is an expression of my inner joy.
I love myself; therefore, I take loving care of my body.
I lovingly feed it nourishing foods and beverages.
I lovingly groom it and dress it,
and my body lovingly responds to me with vibrant health and energy.
I love myself; therefore, I provide for myself a comfortable home,
one that fills all my needs and is a pleasure to be in.
I fill the rooms with the vibrations of love so that all who enter,
myself included, will feel this love and be nourished by it.
I love myself; therefore, I work at a job that I truly enjoy doing,
one that uses my creative talents and abilities working with and
for people I love and who love me and earning a good income.
I love myself; therefore, I behave and think in a loving way
to all people, for I know that which I give out
returns to me multiplied.
I attract only loving people into my world
for they are a mirror of what I am.

I love myself; therefore, I forgive and totally release the past
and all past experiences and I am free.
I love myself; therefore, I love totally in the now,
experiencing each moment as good,
and knowing that my future
is bright and joyous and secure
for I am a beloved child of the universe
and the universe lovingly takes care of me
now and forever more.
All is well in my world.

And so it is.

If you want more...
we offer the following–

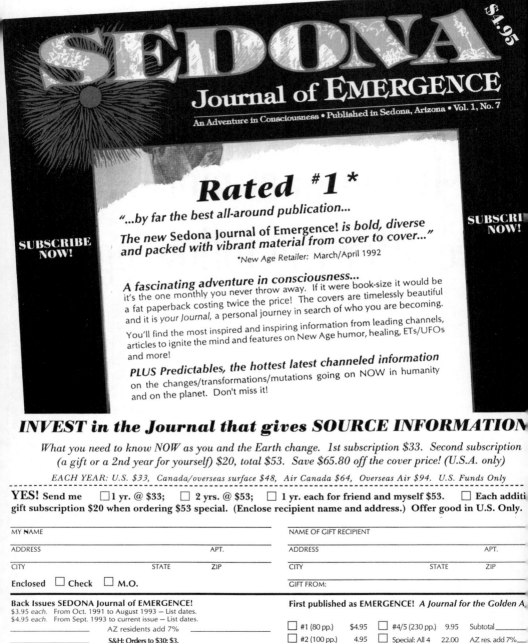

SEDONA
Journal of EMERGENCE
An Adventure in Consciousness • Published in Sedona, Arizona • Vol. 1, No. 7

$4.95

SUBSCRIBE NOW!

SUBSCRI NOW!

Rated #1 *

"...by far the best all-around publication...

The new Sedona Journal of Emergence! is bold, diverse and packed with vibrant material from cover to cover..."

New Age Retailer: March/April 1992

A fascinating adventure in consciousness... it's the one monthly you never throw away. If it were book-size it would be a fat paperback costing twice the price! The covers are timelessly beautiful and it is *your Journal*, a personal journey in search of who you are becoming.

You'll find the most inspired and inspiring information from leading channels, articles to ignite the mind and features on New Age humor, healing, ETs/UFOs and more!

PLUS Predictables, the hottest latest channeled information on the changes/transformations/mutations going on NOW in humanity and on the planet. Don't miss it!

INVEST in the Journal that gives SOURCE INFORMATION

What you need to know NOW as you and the Earth change. 1st subscription $33. Second subscription (a gift or a 2nd year for yourself) $20, total $53. Save $65.80 off the cover price! (U.S.A. only)

EACH YEAR: U.S. $33, Canada/overseas surface $48, Air Canada $64, Overseas Air $94. U.S. Funds Only

- -

YES! Send me ☐ 1 yr. @ $33; ☐ 2 yrs. @ $53; ☐ 1 yr. each for friend and myself $53. ☐ Each additi gift subscription $20 when ordering $53 special. (Enclose recipient name and address.) Offer good in U.S. Only.

MY NAME			NAME OF GIFT RECIPIENT		
ADDRESS		APT.	ADDRESS		APT.
CITY	STATE	ZIP	CITY	STATE	ZIP

Enclosed ☐ Check ☐ M.O.

GIFT FROM:

Back Issues SEDONA Journal of EMERGENCE!
$3.95 each. From Oct. 1991 to August 1993 — List dates.
$4.95 each. From Sept. 1993 to current issue — List dates.

	AZ residents add 7%
	S&H: Orders to $30: $3.
	Over $30: 10% of order.

Enclosed: Check ☐ M.O. ☐ **TOTAL** $ _____

First published as EMERGENCE! *A Journal for the Golden A*

☐ #1 (80 pp.)	$4.95	☐ #4/5 (230 pp.)	9.95	Subtotal	_____
☐ #2 (100 pp.)	4.95	☐ Special: All 4	22.00	AZ res. add 7%	_____
☐ #3 (155 pp.)	5.95			*Ship. & Hand.	_____

*Orders to $30: $3. Over $30 add 10% of order. TOTAL $ _____

MAIL TO: SEDONA Journal of EMERGENCE! • P.O. BOX 1526, Sedona, AZ 86339

BOOK MARKET

A reader's guide to the extraordinary books we publish, print and market for your enLightenment.

NEW!
CHANNELING: Evolutionary Exercises for Channels
by Vywamus through Barbara Burns

A lucid step-by-step guide for experiencd or aspiring chan-... Opens the Self to Source with ...le yet profoundly effective exercises. ...ttorney in Vancouver, Barbara has ...ked with Vywamus since 1987.

...5 Softcover
0-929385-35-7

NEW!
THE EXPLORER RACE
Robert Shapiro
A channeled book.

In this expansive overview, Zoosh, explains "You are the Explorer Race. Learn about your journey before coming to this Earth, your evolution here and what lies ahead." Topics range from ETs, UFOs to relationships.

$24.95 Softcover 650 pp.
ISBN 0-929385-38-1

NEW!
THE NEW AGE PRIMER
Spiritual Tools For Awakening

A guidebook to the changing reality, it is an overview of the concepts and techniques of mastery by authorities in their field. Explores reincarnation, belief systems, and transformative tools from astrology to crystals.

$11.95
ISBN 0-929385-27-6

THE SEDONA VORTEX GUIDEBOOK

200-plus pages of channeled, never-before-published information on ...vortex energies of Sedona — and the ...niques to enable you to use the vor-...s as multidimensional portals to ..., space and other realities.

...95 Softcover 236 pp.
0-929-385-25-X

BOOKS BY WES BATEMAN

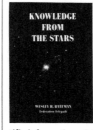

NEW!
KNOWLEDGE FROM THE STARS
by Wes Bateman

A telepath with contact to ETs, Bateman has provided a wide spectrum of scientific information. A fascinating compilation of articles surveying the Federation, ETs, evolution, and the trading houses, all part of the true history of the galaxy.

$11.95 Softcover ISBN 0-929385-39-X

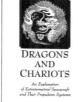

DRAGONS AND CHARIOTS
by Wes Bateman

An explanation of spacecraft, propulsion systems, gravity, the Dragon, manipulated Light, interstellar & intergalactic motherships by renowned telepath who details specific technological information he has been given in contact with ETs.

$9.95 Softcover ISBN 0-929385-26-8

...OKS BY DR. HEATHER ANNE HARDER

NEW!
EXPLORING LIFE'S LAST FRONTIER
by Dr. Heather Anne Harder

By becoming familiar with death, the amount of fear ...grief will be reduced, making the ...sition and transformation of Earth ...e joyful. A manual for learning ac-...ance and letting go.

...95 Softcover 315 pp.
1-881343-03-0

MANY WERE CALLED — FEW WERE CHOSEN
by Dr. Heather Anne Harder

The story of Terra (Earth) from the beginning — its mission, and the volunteers who were sent to rescue that mission. Uncovers the mystery of our origins.

$9.95 Softcover 89 pp.
ISBN 0-929385-34-9

NEW!
TALKS WITH JONATHON Book I
As told to Robin Miller

The limited past perception of what is real and unreal is soon to be altered. With clarity and compassion, Jonathon sets forth guidelines for those on the path of self-mastery in this changing time.

$14.95 softcover 160 pp.
ISBN 1-81343-04-9

BOOK MARKET

BOOK MARKET

BOOKS BY TOM DONGO

NEW!
THE QUEST
The Mysteries of Sedona III
by Tom Dongo

Fascinating stories of 26 who [hea]rd the call to Sedona; Tom Dongo's [col]umns, *UFOs, ETs and You*; and pic[tur]es of the area.

[19]95 Softcover 144 pp.
[ISB]N 0-9622748-2-8

THE ALIEN TIDE
The Mysteries of Sedona II
by Tom Dongo

UFO-ET, metaphysical and paranormal activity in Sedona, Arizona, and nationwide, with a strong focus on UFO and alien activity. Photos and illustrations.

$7.95 Softcover 128 pp.
ISBN 0-9622748-1-X

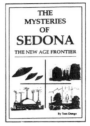

THE MYSTERIES OF SEDONA
by Tom Dongo

An overview of the New Age Mecca that is Sedona, Arizona. Topics are the famous energy vortexes, UFOs, channeling, Lemuria, metaphysical and mystical experiences and area paranormal activity. Photos and illustrations.

$6.95 Softcover 84 pp.
ISBN 0-96227480-0-1

THE MONTAUK PROJECT
Experiments in Time
by Preston B. Nichols with Peter Moon

The truth about time that reads like science fiction! Secret [rese]arch with invisibility experiments [th]at culminated at Montauk, tapping the [po]wers of creation and manipulating [tim]e itself. Exposé by the engineer who [serv]ed as technical director.

[$1]5.95 Softcover 160 pp.
[ISB]N 0-9631889-0-9

BOOKS BY BRIAN GRATTAN

Brian Grattan

MAHATMA
by Brian Grattan

An explanation of mankind's eternal journey for those motivated to search beyond old theologies and belief systems for final enlightenment. With special techniques and meditations to assist you in creating your spiritual Lightbody for Ascension.

$14.95 Softcover 276 pp.
ISBN 0-929385-26-8

Brian Grattan

NEW!
MAHATMA II
by Brian Grattan

Guidance to reach an evolutionary level of integration for conscious ascension. Fascinating diagrams and illustrations, exercises and meditations. Information and conversations with Mahatma, the I AM Presence.

$14.95 Softcover 328 pp.
ISBN 0-929385-46-2

BOOKS BY ROYAL/PRIEST

PRISM OF LYRA
by Lyssa Royal and Keith Priest

Traces the inception of the human race back to Lyra, [wh]ere the original expansion of duality [i]s begun, to be finally integrated on [Ea]rth.

[$1]1.95 Softcover 112 pp.
[IS]BN 0-9631320-0-8

VISITORS FROM WITHIN
by Lyssa Royal and Keith Priest

Explores the extraterrestrial contact and abduction phenomenon in a unique and intriguing way. A combination of narrative, precisely-focused channeled material and firsthand accounts.

$12.95 Softcover 171 pp.
ISBN 0-9631320-1-6

NEW!
THE GOLDEN PATH
Channeled by **Ruth Ryden**

A "Book of Lessons" by the master teachers explaining the process of channeling, Akashic records, karma, opening the third eye, the ego and the meaning of Bible stories. It is a master class for aquiring spiritual concepts and opening your personal pathway.

$11.95 Softcover
ISBN 0-929385-42-X

BOOK MARKET

BOOKS BY ELWOOD BABBITT

NEW!
PERFECT HEALTH
by Elwood Babbitt

For the first time ever, the world's most respected names in medicine and science speak through the noted trans-medium addressing health and lifestyle issues. Wilhelm Reich, Eintstein and others offer opinions on AIDS, abortion, nutrition and the purpose of Life. Rewarding reading!

$15.95 Softcover 297pp.
ISBN 1-881343-01-4

VOICES OF SPIRIT
by Elwood Babbitt and Charles H. Hapgood

The author discusses 15 years of work with Elwood Babbitt. This book will fascinate both the curious sceptic and the believer. Includes complete transcripts.

$13.00 Softcover 350 pp.
ISBN 1-881343-00-6

NEW!
LIVING RAINBOWS
by Gabriel H. Bain

A fascinating 'how-to' manual to make experiencing human, astral, animal and plant auras an everyday event. Series of techniques, exercises and illustrations guide the serious student or the simply curious to see *and hear* aural energy. Spiral-bound workbook format.

$14.95 Softcover
ISBN 0-929385-43-8

THE GOD WITHIN
A Testament Of Vishnu
by Elwood Babbitt & Charles Hapgood

A handbook for the spiritual renaissance. Testifies to the unlimited potential of trance communication and of our own inner awakenings in dialogue format.

$12.95 Hardcover 359 pp.

BOOKS BY ALOA STARR

NEW EDIT
PRISONER OF EARTH
Psychic Possession and its Release
by Aloa Sta

The sympto causes and release tech ques in a do mented exploration by a practitioner. fascinating study that de-mystfies the phenomenon of possession and offers "patients" new hope.

$11.95 Softcover 179 pp.
ISBN 0-929385-37-3

NEW!
I WANT TO KNOW
by Aloa Starr

A book for children and adults. It delights young minds and off answers to stir their awakenir From "Why am I here?" to "Who is God?"

$7.00 Softcover 87 pp.
ISBN 0-929686-02-0

BOOKS BY LYNN BUESS

CHILDREN OF LIGHT; CHILDREN OF DENIAL
by Lynn Buess, M.A.,Ed.S.

In his fourth book, Lynn calls upon his decades of practice as counselor and psychotherapist to explore the relationship between karma and the new insights from ACOA/Co-dependency writings.

$8.95 Softcover 125 pp.
ISBN 0-929385-15-2

NUMEROLOGY: NUANCES IN RELATION-SHIPS
by Lynn Buess, M.A.,Ed.S.

Provides valuable assistance in the quest to better understand compatabilities and conflicts with a significant other. With a handy guide for calculating your/his/her personality numbers.

$12.65 Softcover 239 pp.
ISBN 0-929385-23-3

NUMEROLOGY FOR THE NEW AGE
by Lynn Buess, M.A., Ed.S.

An established standard, explic ing for contemporary readers ancient art and science of symbol, cycle, and vibration Provides insights into the patterns of our personal lives. Includes Life and sonality Numbers.

$9.85 Softcover 262 pp.
ISBN 0-929385-31-4

BOOK MARKET